INGER PALMSTIERNA

Practical Rose Gardening

HOW TO PLACE, PLANT, AND GROW MORE THAN FIFTY EASY-CARE VARIETIES

Translated by Gun Penhoat

Skyhorse Publishing

Copyright © 2008 Inger Palmstierna and Prisma, Stockholm
First published by Bokförlaget Prisma, an imprint of Norstedts, Sweden, in 2008 as Rosor: i vackert sällskap by Inger Palmstierna. Published by agreement with Norstedts Agency.

English language edition copyright © 2015 by Skyhorse Publishing, Inc.

Skyhorse Publishing books may be purchased in bulk at special discounts for sales promotion, corporate gifts, fund-raising, or educational purposes. Special editions can also be created to specifications. For details, contact the Special Sales Department, Skyhorse Publishing, 307 West 36th Street, 11th Floor, New York, NY 10018 or info @skyhorsepublishing.com.

Skyhorse® and Skyhorse Publishing® are registered trademarks of Skyhorse Publishing, Inc.®, a Delaware corporation.

Visit our website at www.skyhorsepublishing.com.

10 9 8 7 6 5 4 3 2 1

Library of Congress Cataloging-in-Publication Data is available on file.

Cover design by Lottie & Jonas Hallqvist, Graffoto AB
Cover photo credit by Inger Palmstierna

Print ISBN: 978-1-62914-740-6
Ebook ISBN: 978-1-63220-094-5

Printed in China

FOREWORD

Yet another book devoted to roses might elicit sighs from some readers, as there are already plenty of publications on the topic in print. However, this book is different from others. While it deals with roses, to be sure, this book's emphasis is on how to use roses in a wide variety of settings, rather than simply being a collection of individual rose portraits.

As one might expect, a flower of such renown has had a lot written about it. Even as a child, I turned the pages of the Dutch advertising catalogs again and again, drawn in by the beautiful pictures of the flowers within. So you can imagine my disappointment when, in the 1970s, I began working in a garden center, and realized that the stark-blue dream rose 'Mainzer Fastnacht' resembled a washed-out dishcloth, the deep red 'Hanne' wilted quickly into a faded violet, and the orange 'Super Star' was more salmon pink than brightly fluorescent orange.

As the assortment of roses available on the market is constantly in flux, there's no doubt that a new book on this flower was in order. While there are plenty of portraits of roses in catalogs and product brochures, this book emphasizes how to incorporate them into different garden environments. It also highlights new and healthy species, the especially hardy ones, new bare-root roses and delicate specimens for the south of Sweden. This, along with advice on how to care for the rose, to make it bloom bountifully, and turn it into a low-maintenance part of the garden instead of a plant in need of constant coddling, is the aim of this book. It is an overall guide on the care, use, and choice of roses.

It's easy to fall under the spell of roses. You find yourself entranced by beautiful pictures, only to choose a variety that might not work for you at all. This book covers the whole country and describes roses specifically suited to Sweden—what's possible to grow in beds and/or in combinations. All pictures, with a few exceptions, are taken in Sweden. Knowledgeable and clear advice about irrigation, pruning and diseases is all here. Information is somewhat limited on historic or old-fashioned garden roses, so if you'd like to learn more about these types of flowers, there are other more comprehensive volumes that I gladly recommend you seek out. The display of roses,

their suitability to different settings, and examples of successful companion plants are also an important part of this book.

I still have favorite, stand-by roses, and many can be found within these pages. I also cover many varieties that are largely untried in Sweden as of yet.

Here is some food for thought. On the clamor for better, more tried, and hardier varieties, I cite Svend Poulsen from his book, *Roses*:

"There was a time when all roses had to have large, petal-rich blossoms; that was the style in the late nineteenth century and it continued well into the twentieth. I'm not denying that old-fashioned roses are beautiful—far from it; but it's also true that tastes evolve.

It was the light, elegant, and pointy flowers of the tea roses that changed the fashion, and opened rose cultivators' eyes to a whole new world of beauty. Unfortunately, those roses were unable to satisfy all the requirements asked of them—their canes were too pliable and weak, and the flower wasn't hardy enough. It seemed, however, that hybrid tea roses, a sound and sturdy rose specimen, might be able to meet all that was demanded of a rose, but a long time would pass before this development was accomplished. It didn't happen until after 1930, and it was first with the single-blossom polyantha roses that this type of rose experienced a breakthrough—that the simple varieties were finally accepted as a rose for one's garden and that they could bring pleasure."

Svend Poulsen, who worked in the family enterprise Poulsen's Roses that launched many of the world's most famous roses, wrote the above in 1941.

His opinion is critical of the old-fashioned, gaudy, full-blown roses. They were popular, and his customers—hobbyist gardeners—didn't want simple, single-bloom roses, which at the time were the newest and healthiest of roses. By reprinting this quote, I want to show to you that there are fads even in the world of plants, and that you sometimes need to look past fashion in order to find the plants that will flourish in your own garden.

Inger Palmstierna

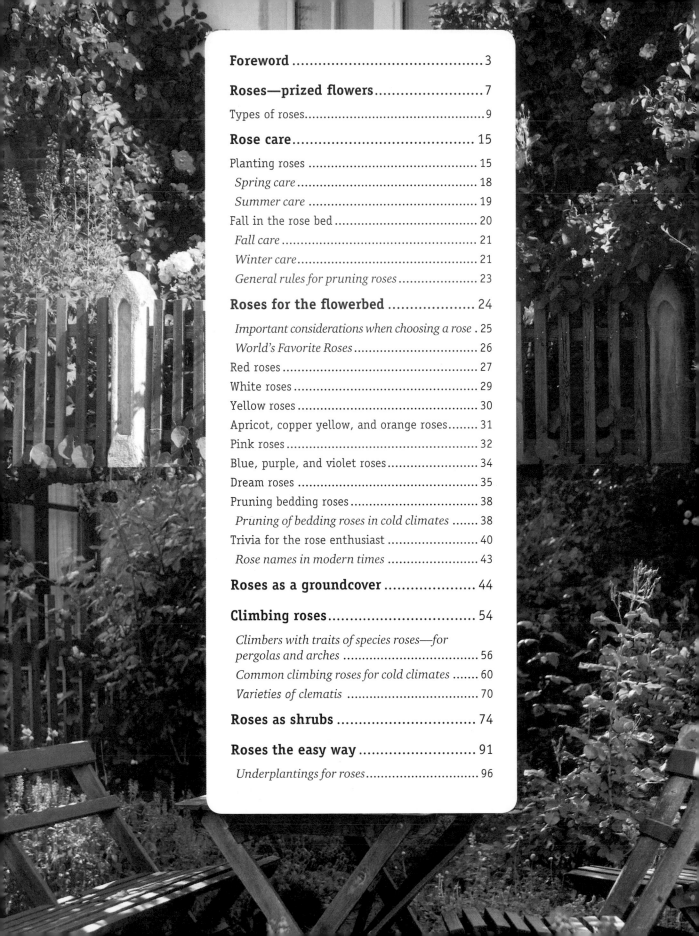

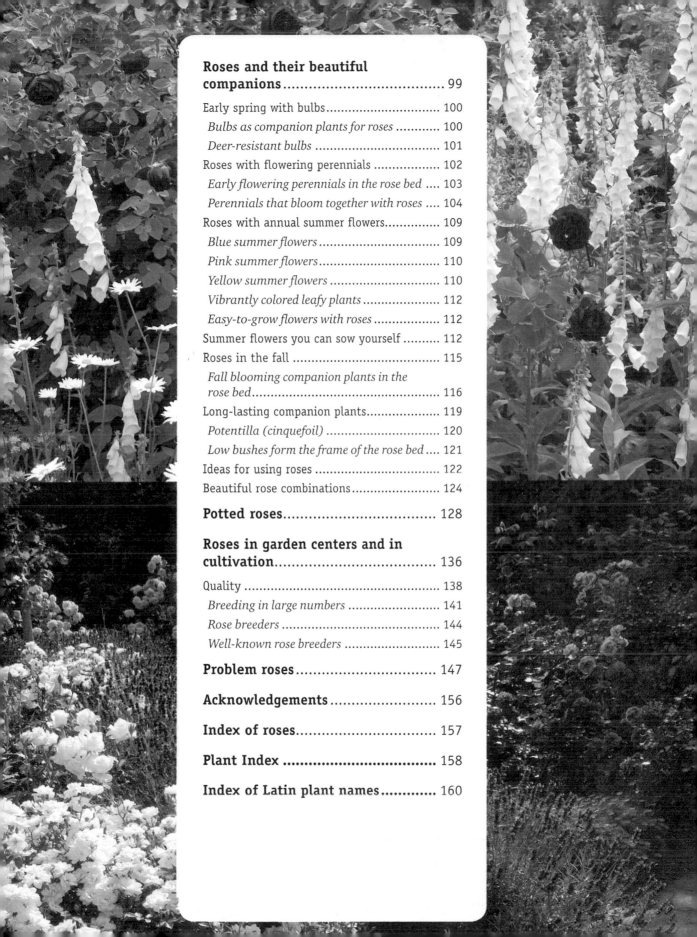

A rose dream.

ROSES— PRIZED FLOWERS

Many gardeners love to grow roses; for many of them, roses stand for so much more than a mere flower. They symbolize love, and they're also historically significant. The rose has many advantages, one of which is the fact that no other perennial blooms as abundantly and over such a long time in the flowerbed (modern roses typically are in flower from early summer until the snow falls). There are roses for all occasions—if the planting site is sunny—and they bloom in all imaginable colors except true blue.

Roses are naturally wonderful and multi-faceted plants. Those that we cultivate in our gardens have their origins in species of wild roses. They can be small and hug the ground, or they can be large or more liana-like, climbing high up into the treetops. Roses are found all over the world—there are species originating in Asia, Europe, and North America. Their appearance varies widely, and they each possess their own set of characteristics. To derive the most enjoyment out of the flower, it's best to choose the right rose for the intended place and purpose.

A Plant With History

Cultivating roses is an ancient practice; people have grown them for thousands of years. Over time, the especially beautiful specimens—those with the headiest fragrance, the most dazzling and unusual colors, or longest-blooming flowers— were selected for breeding. The petals were the basis for medicines, essential oils, and perfumes, as well as for food, wine, and decoration.

There are around one hundred and fifty species of wild roses, and it's believed that seven of them are at the origin of today's modern roses. Roses are quite promiscuous—different varieties will breed with each other and produce new varieties. Roses can even spontaneously mutate and create a new variety. In this case it is said that the rose has produced a 'sport.' This sport in turn can produce its own, new sport. Because of increased breeding roses are quite 'unstable,' which means that a new kind of rose can suddenly appear in the home garden.

An array of modern roses

Rose varieties increase in number every year, and thus new, beautiful flowers are regularly introduced. Many of them are still unknown in Sweden but deserve to be shown. Roses from the 1960s and earlier are still the most common roses found in our gardens and garden centers, but much progress has taken place over the past 50 years of breeding. Today, modern roses are fragrant while keeping their charming old-world shapes, and are available in many colors. They flower longer than their ancestors, and in tones only dreamt of in the 1800s when rose hysteria was at its peak. New types of roses have been introduced, such as low climbers, ramblers for pillars and posts, and spreading groundcovers in a variety of forms. Do not peruse this book hoping to spot old favorites, as it covers mostly new varieties—and even so, due to the vast scale of the subject matter, only a selected few of these recent arrivals (out of the many worth cultivating) are mentioned herein.

Old garden roses or modern roses

Over the past few years Sweden has experienced a resurgent yet somewhat newfangled interest in old-fashioned roses. It's not just us, either: modern-day society seems to seek out vibrantly colored and multi-petal large-flowered roses. This is no different from the past, when the desire for stripy, large-bloom, richly hued roses was so strong that scent or concern for plant health and hardiness was largely ignored. As early as in the 1870s, a single flower's appearance took precedence over its other characteristics. The old-garden rose we think of as 'traditional' is in fact more loved and used today than it ever was in the past. Price lists and lists of roses from the late 1800s up until around the 1970s indicate that there were very few old garden roses for sale. Of those available then, many are no longer available or mentioned due to their inferior quality. Yet other roses available then are basically identical to the current old-garden roses that are blockbusters today.

Proper classification of roses states that any rose existing prior to 1867 be placed in the Old Garden Rose class, even if the variety is new. All others are classified as modern roses. Origin, category and methods of classification are of interest to both rose scientists and hobbyists. The two camps are not always in agreement, contributing to many a discussion about which rose belongs to what category. DNA analysis complicates matters further, as old beliefs and practices become obsolete when new facts emerge.

In the past, the colors of rose beds were nearly always red, white, or rose. These older types of roses, dating back to the 1900s, belong to the group called 'modern roses'. They flower continuously throughout the summer, unlike many of the 'old-garden roses' that often flower only once or twice.

The many beautiful features of roses

To cultivate roses successfully, you'll need to plan how you want to use them, since growing a rose hedge, a rose-covered pergola, or a rose bed all require different kinds of roses. By choosing the right rose, you can use them to embellish your garden or balcony, or plant them in containers placed in a sunny spot on your deck or patio.

Simple care instructions and good soil will soon turn your garden into a flowering oasis with happy bumblebees buzzing around the fragrant flowers, which will blossom throughout the summer. With this in mind, I have divided the book into sections—not from a botanical perspective, but from a practical standpoint—to illustrate how and

Modern roses now exist in colors that were not yet conceived in the 1800s, when the interest in rose gardening was at its peak.

The simple 'Cherry Meidiland' and the hybrid tea rose 'Black Baccara' with large blooms illustrate two completely different flower forms, both beautiful in their own way.

A typical bedding rose, new in the 1930s, planted and proudly shown off by its owner.

what roses are best used in various settings, much in the way those sections are set up in a garden center or plant nursery.

Types of roses

Roses for flowerbeds

'Bedding rose' is the collective term for roses suitable to use in rose beds. Among them are multiflora sprays and large-flowered roses, as well as many modern shrub roses. Sprays have many flowers growing in clusters or bouquets, and impart lots of color to the rose bed. Large-flowering varieties feature big blooms, with one or two at the top of the shoot. The flower is impressive but doesn't offer quite the same vibrant color effect as the multiflora sprays. Both types of roses are pruned hard in springtime to keep them at a proper low height.

'Modern shrub rose' is a somewhat fuzzy and generic botanical term that includes heterogeneous groups of roses featuring a bush-like growth pattern, as well as roses that don't belong to any other specific group. However, only a few of them are large-flowering, and can—if the canes overwinter—become shrubs. The English Austin rose and the headily fragrant Renaissance rose are found among the shrub roses. Most modern shrub roses are perfect for flowerbeds.

'Ingrid Bergman', a typical and very popular bedding rose in the 1900s that's still a big seller today.

A simple way to grow roses is to use them as groundcover. It is common practice today, but its popularity in the home and hobby garden started back in the 1980s. Different kinds have taken off, but the most common variety is 'The Fairy' from 1932.

Climbing roses, unlike clematis, have no special tendrils for attachment. The prickles can interlace, but the canes should be tied up against a support for a more attractive finish.

Groundcover roses

Roses that cover the ground have long, trailing canes and sprawling growth habits. They're used on slopes, in borders and as groundcover in public space plantings to prevent weeds. Their main characteristic is that they're wider than they are high. They don't necessarily hug the ground—some are pillow-like while others make a low, wide funnel. The shoots often grow straight up first before reclining. There are lower, creeping roses, and also more cascading types. Interest in groundcover roses has increased markedly over the past twenty years, along with a general desire for an easier-to-care-for garden.

Climbing roses

Climbing roses grow long, supple canes. They have no tendrils to use for upward mobility, but can hook their canes' prickles (thorns) in order to grow vertically. If they're not trained against any kind of support, they will spread sideways. Some are sturdier (and usually non-repeaters, like 'New Dawn') and are suitable for pergolas and arches. Others, lower to the ground and featuring more elegant, repeating blooms, are perfect on a trellis or latticework against a wall. Some can be used as a large shrub, or can be trained as a smaller climber against a vertical support.

Shrub roses

Included in this section are the groups 'park roses' and 'shrub roses'. They can be repeat-blooming, non-repeaters, or they can bloom abundantly once and then again more sparsely in late summer, in which case they are called 'remontant'. This group includes many of the very popular old garden roses. In spite of being called shrub roses, they can be both large and small. Some, like *Rosa pimpinnelifolia* (burnet or Scots rose), can turn into large shrubs, while others get no bigger than a sturdy flowerbed rose. Most rugosa roses, such as *Rosa rubiginosa* and the Japanese rose, also belong to this group. Shrub roses are lightly pruned—they only need to be neatened up in the same way as a lilac or a mock orange bush.

Several roses grown together are even more beautiful. A climbing rose, probably 'Flammentanz', is given some shadow around its roots by the low-growing 'Fru Dagmar Hastrup', a variety that is often used as a groundcover in problem areas.

Roses called 'shrub roses' can come in large sizes or small varieties suitable for flowerbeds. You'll need to find out their size and hardiness to get a rose that will readily grow into a shrub.

Many of the larger-sized park or shrub roses make excellent hedges. They're planted like other flowering hedges, but their prickles add extra protection from intrusion. Count on a rose hedge to grow rather wide. A flowering hedge is only pruned sparingly.

Some shrub roses are beautiful planted as hedges. Rosa rugosa is an excellent choice for windy areas where many other plants might not thrive.

Roses that thrive in pots

There are several kinds of roses that thrive in pots. Small miniature roses sold as houseplants can be used the same way as bedding plants, and small bedding roses are perfect for cultivation as perennials in containers. There are varieties with normal-sized flowers and leaves, and ones with smaller flowers and leaves. Potted roses need extra protection in winter and are pruned hard.

Many roses can be grown in pots, but there are also specially bred rose varieties raised just for pots.

Try many roses

Many new roses are introduced each year, and there is always at least one worth trying out. When it comes to roses, the adage 'old is better' is not true—quite the opposite in fact. New varieties have superior flower power, stronger fragrance, and tend to be more disease resistant. Over the past decade, rose breeders have put a lot of effort into producing new roses with old rose fragrance.

First, roses should be carefully selected with their location and function in mind. The next critical step is the choice of color. In the section 'Roses for the flowerbed,' p. 24, you will find them sorted by color. No matter what the type of rose, color can vary enormously between the pictured flower and what is described in the text, so if the color of the rose is an essential factor, you will have to try to get a look at a real specimen.

Your chosen variety of rose should be disease resistant. A delicate rose is more difficult to care for and will require a lot more upkeep than a hardy specimen. This is a strong argument for choosing to plant newer varieties.

Take the time to try out several different new roses. They're generally affordable, so indulge by planting many of them together. Also, it's not always necessary to pay attention to the type of rose or to which 'botanical classification' it belongs—don't let words such as hybrid tea rose, large-flowered climber, *wichuraiana* rose (memorial rose) or *Rosa rugosa* make you nervous!

You can dig up, exchange, and move roses without any trouble during the spring and fall seasons. Planting can be done from early spring to late fall. If the outcome is unsatisfactory, roses can be potted and left in the garden to grow further, where you can keep an eye on them and see if they improve. If the color is not to your liking, roses can be moved to another flowerbed.

Roses are not fragile and delicate ladies—quite the opposite—they're hardy and robust plants. What they do need is good and porous soil, sun, and plenty of water and nutrients. There are no roses that thrive in the shade, contrary to what some people may have you believe. This information is only relevant to those who live in much warmer climes, with longer summers, than in northern Europe. In Sweden, roses need a sunny spot for at least half the day. The area needn't be a sun-drenched south-facing site—east or west is just as acceptable.

Roses are not fragile, but they do require a sunny spot in good soil with plenty of water and nutrients. In order to flower generously throughout the summer, they need more water and nutrients than other plants; then again, they do flower so much more than other flowers.

ROSE CARE

No plants flower so abundantly and over such a long period of time as roses do. Consequently, they require a bit more care than say, lilacs, which typically bloom only once and then go dormant. To grow and to flower generously, roses need plenty of water and nutrients; they can be compared to elite athletes who need more energy to produce top results than what most regular folks need to go jogging around the block a few times. To get good results, you have to provide your roses with what they need to produce plenty of flowers.

Planting roses

All roses like a sunny spot with good soil. Typically, roses are planted in the spring, but it's perfectly okay to plant container-grown roses from early spring through late fall. Planting bare-root roses can be done in early spring and late fall—see 'Roses in garden centers and in cultivation,' p. 136. No matter what type of roses or how they are sold, their planting method is the same.

The soil needs to be loose to allow the roots to grow and develop easily. You can amend the soil where you want to set the flowers by digging large planting holes, and mixing the ground soil with equal amounts of compost or commercial soil. The hole should be 50 cm (20") deep and equally wide. Keep in mind that thorough soil preparation makes for less maintenance later on.

Plant the rose deep in the ground, leaving the bud union (also called the graft—see photo) at least 5 cm (2"), preferably 10 cm (4") below the soil's surface; the lower parts of the green branches will then also be below the surface. The planting hole must be deep enough so the roots can hang freely, straight down, without bending. The roots should not bend upwards—it's better to trim them a little before planting them to prevent that from happening. A bare-root plant has to stand in a bucket of water for a few hours before being planted, and container-grown roses also need to be properly irrigated.

Remove the container, plastic bag, or netting, and lower the plant into its prepared, ample space; fill the hole with water. When the water has been completely absorbed by the soil and while keeping the plant upright, fill the hole back in with soil and then water once more. Fill the space generously with soil, covering up some of the rose branches, and tamp it down once with your feet on each side of the rose to make sure the plant is settled in securely. If planted in spring, the rose needs to be pruned hard—when in the ground, all visible branches are pruned to 10 to 20 cm (4" to 8") above ground level. This makes the rose branch out and produce many new shoots from the lower part of the plant. If you don't prune the rose, it will grow taller but with fewer and stragglier branches.

Most roses don't grow from their own-root, but on the root of another rose—a stock plant. The bud union is where the new rose is grafted onto the stock, where brown root and green branches meet.

Roses are mostly sold in containers. *Loosen the soil in the spring and weed.* *Add new soil each year as the soil erodes with time.*

Roses thrive when pruned because doing so strengthens them and makes them grow sturdy. A rose in leaf isn't pruned until the following spring, but if it's lanky or ugly looking, then there's no harm in pruning it—quite the opposite.

Change out the soil

If you've already grown roses in the spot where you'd like to plant your new flowers, it's a good idea to replace the soil. Roses can be affected by 'rose plant disorder' and this remains in the soil where roses have been grown before.

As usual, dig a large hole and place the soil in a wheelbarrow. Then take some soil for the new rose from another section of the garden, and mix this soil with an equal amount of compost or purchased soil. The old soil that you've dug up is not poisonous or unusable, but it's not suitable for roses anymore; it can instead be added to another flowerbed or can be used to fill in where the new soil was taken.

If you're changing out a whole rose bed, it's critical to remove the old soil. Take out the dirt until the bed looks like a ditch. Prepare the new soil with an equal amount of compost or purchased soil, and use it to fill in the ditch.

Compost is especially good for amending beds because it works against rose plant disorder. It's a good idea to add some cow manure to it too, as it's mild and acts as an amendment. Half of the amended soil ought to be garden soil, though—if you use only compost or commercial soil, it will sink in and shrink down too much. Specialty bagged rose soil containing clay and nutrients can be used instead of compost.

A protruding roof line

If you plant your rose by the exterior of a house, you'll need to make sure to plant it at some distance from the wall. No matter how the house is built, it's always very dry near walls, which is not good for the rose and will make the flower difficult to care for. However, a rose bed along the wall is beautiful to behold, so fool the eye by placing the bed 40 to 50 cm (16½" to 19½") out from the wall, and lay a path out of stone slabs or gravel behind the bed. That way the roses avoid droughts, their soil drains better, and there won't be any dirt splashing against the side of the house. When you stand in front of the house, you won't notice the path between the house and the rose bed.

A width of about 50 to 70 cm (19½" to 27½") provides plenty of room for a simple bed. If you're digging a whole rose bed in one go, you can make the job easier by digging a wide ditch that you'll fill in with amended soil. You'll have easier access for planting, the roots will have ample space in the prepped soil, and the bed will be easier to maintain. First plant the roses, then add more soil, and then add smaller plants to the loosened soil between the roses.

Rose fertilizer

There are several kinds of fertilizer specifically for roses on the market, and while you don't have to buy any of these products, it's not a bad idea to give them a try. In Sweden, Chrysan is an organic fertilizer that can be used on most garden plants. It's slow-release and is used to fertilize flowers in the spring to ensure abundant blooms. If you use regular commercial fertilizer instead, you'll need to administer it several times over the summer, as the nutrients in those fertilizers are easily dissolved but don't stay in the soil for very long. Long-acting fertilizer like Chrysan, or any other natural fertilizer, only needs to be applied once in the spring.

You can also water your flowers with liquid fertilizer. One ml of the Swedish fertilizer Blomstra (or local equivalent) per quart of water is excellent for roses as well as for all other plants in the garden. The concentration I've suggested here is weaker than what is recommended on the packaging, but if it's administered each time the plants are irrigated, the roses will have a regular supply of food and will reward you with lots of flowers.

The rose bed in spring

The care of the garden's roses begins in spring. They might have needed a protective covering during winter—it all depends on the climate and weather. If the roses have been covered—see p. 21—you'll need to uncover them,

Do not plant roses under a protruding roof. Place a row of stone slabs or gravel near the wall and plant the roses 50 cm (19½") out from the wall. This is better for the siding and the roses, and it helps with drainage.

taking care not to do this too early in the season. When the spring sun is out it can seem warm and intense, yet there might still be night frost, which can quickly freeze many roses to death. The worst damage typically takes place in late winter and early spring—the rose's branches can cope with the winter cold, but not with the contrast of warm days and ice cold nights—so hold back on baring the roses until spring has really taken hold and the weather has stabilized. There's isn't a surefire date for this, as it could mean March in the south of Sweden, while further north it might be in May, depending on how early or late spring arrives. The pruning of roses should take place in early spring—see p. 19.

Loosen the soil

The dirt that you stacked up around the roses in the fall to protect them from the elements now needs to be raked away. Take this opportunity to weed thoroughly and loosen up the soil with a small handheld hoe. The soil's surface becomes hard and crusty over winter and needs to be broken up to allow for rain and water to trickle down into the ground. Take care to hoe only the surface so you don't inadvertently damage the rose's roots. This is also the time to spread fertilizer and add more soil or soil amendments. The amendments can be in the form of plant soil, cow manure, compost, or enriched soil. Fertilizer can be mixed into the soil amendment that is spread on the flowerbed.

Weeds will start growing before the roses have a chance to wake up, so the earlier you start weeding, the easier it will be to keep on top of the weeds, and the prettier you rose beds will be. If you've put down a weed barrier fabric around the roses, you'll only need to pull the weeds and the moss that grow on the fabric and in the planting holes. Avoid trampling the rose bed, as the soil needs to stay as loose as possible.

Irrigation

Roses need water during the summer, and preparing for regular irrigation should be done in the spring. It needs to be a very rainy summer indeed to get away with not watering, since roses need at least 30 mm (1.18") of rain per week, which is equivalent to 7½ gallons per 1 m² (10.18 sq ft) of rose bed.

A good investment is to buy an irrigation hose—either a soaker hose or drip line. The hose can be set down in the spring to avoid damaging the plants. It's coiled around the roses so that each rose has a bit of hose near it—the rose foliage shields the hose from view. If the soil is covered with a weed barrier fabric, simply place the soaker hose or drip line on top of it. The fabric lets the water through, albeit at a slightly slower pace than if the hose were lying directly on the ground. The soaker hose is turned on when the roses need water.

In the summer you'll need to water each week if it doesn't rain. In spring, first check deep down in the soil—it could already be damp, depending on whether the preceding fall and winter were dry or wet. Use a small

Axelina is sunning herself in front of 'Mystic Fairy' (at left) and 'Fairy Dance' (at right).

An irrigation hose is a convenient and efficient way to water. It uses less water but it gets to the roots of the rose where it's needed most, instead of on foliage and flowers.
The rose is 'Linnaeus'.

SPRING CARE

- Remove covers such as banked earth, pine boughs and similar protection.
- Weed thoroughly and loosen up the soil's surface.
- Add soil amended with a slow-release fertilizer.
- Add long-acting fertilizer if not already included in the soil.
- Pruning: roses are pruned depending on type and personal preference—see below for further details on pruning.
- Place irrigation hose between the plants.

hand spade and dig carefully down a little bit to see if the soil is moist. At watering time, let the hose drip through the night—at least 5 to 6 hours if the water pressure is low.

Summer care

You'll get more abundant blooms if you water once a week in the summer. Here, soaking hoses have distinct advantages: they use far less water; all the water reaches the plants' roots; the water seeps slowly into the ground and deep enough to truly help the plant. Water on the soil's surface is of no use to a thirsty rose—it needs to reach down at least 30 to 40 cm (12" to 16") into the ground. Also, by using soaker hoses no water ends up on the driveway, garden furniture or walkway. The plant itself is kept dry, which lessens the risk of fungal diseases that can settle onto damp foliage. The flowers stay dry and exquisite. If you use spray attachment to irrigate the flowers, they might fill with water and rot, or they might become mottled with brown spots or become infected with grey mold.

If extra fertilizer is needed, you can spread it out before turning on the irrigation. If the rose petals look light in color, suddenly develop a strange pattern, or if the plant has an overall hang-dog look to it, it's a good idea to try some additional fertilizer. Liquid fertilizer administered from a watering can will have quicker effect in this case.

Trim and control

You'll have to check over the roses once a week, perhaps at the time you turn on the water. Keep a vigilant eye on the shoots at the top of the plant, as aphids and other pests usually hunker down there. You will also notice if the shoots look pale, eaten, sticky or droopy. If there is a contamination (see 'Problem roses,' p. 147) you'll need to deal with it as soon as possible.

'Bright Cover' is a self-trimming rose—its faded leaves fall to the ground. Roses with big, full blooms often need a bit of help and should have their withered flowers snipped off.

The plant will look much better if you take the time to snip off—deadhead—any faded flowers. Certain roses, especially some of the older ones, flower much more when the withered blooms are removed. Older books and catalogs call this 'to neaten' or 'to tidy.'

Opinions differ on how much to remove when snipping, but if you remove the faded flower and cut down to the first real leaf underneath the flower, the plant will bloom more abundantly next time. It takes approximately 6 weeks from the faded flower's removal to the next flower to come up on the same shoot. These roses are called continuous-blooming. Flower buds that develop rot, dry up or become brown, or fail to open should be snipped off, as they only deplete the plant of strength; if they're removed, new buds will appear far quicker.

If you want to get decorative rosehips, however, don't remove the spent flowers. It's the faded flower that eventually becomes a rosehip, but not all roses will turn into hips. You can cut off the first lot of spent flowers and let the next round of flowers set hips, but this will depend on the length of summer in which the rose is grown. Bedding roses seldom give rose hips—they should be continuously trimmed throughout the summer to encourage rich flowering.

Roses are pruned in the spring—see 'General rules for pruning roses', p. 23—and during the summer the plant grows new shoots. These shoots should be reasonably equal in length, so snip off the shoots that grow out further than the others.

SUMMER CARE
- Water regularly once a week—7½ gallon per 1 m² (10.18 sq ft) of rose bed.
- Snip off spent flowers; trim. This is not necessary, but you will be rewarded with more abundant flowers.
- Try extra fertilizer if the leaves and petals look pale.
- Check for pests and treat as necessary.
- Snip off shoots that grow past the others.

Drooping roses can be rolled up hard in paper—flowers tilted upwards and covered—so they have support of the paper. Set them deeply in water and place them in a cool place overnight. If the roses are fresh enough they might regain the strength to straighten up again.

Roses in bouquets

Bedding roses make excellent cut flowers for bouquets. Choose branches with buds that are starting to open and show color, preferably cut from the stronger canes—thin canes with heavy flowers will often nod. Cut the branch just above a leaf, leaving the leaf on the plant. Make a long, diagonal cut across the stem and immediately place the rose in a vase filled with cold water. The flower itself should be above water while the stem should be submerged as much as possible. Place the vase in a cool place for an hour or two to let the rose draw up some water, then remove leaves that fall into the water, as they will rot and make the rose fade quicker. The rose will last longer if you change the water daily and rinse the stem. If the cut planes on the stems look brown and fuzzy and feel sticky, make a new, fresh cut a bit further up the stem. Long-stemmed roses tend to nod more readily than their short-stemmed counterparts because it's a longer way up for the water to reach the flower.

An ounce of prevention makes for longer lasting roses—a lump of sugar mixed with ⅛ teaspoon of citric acid in a quart of water works well if there is nothing else at hand.

Fall in the rose bed

The leaves on the rose plant start to turn yellow and drop off when fall arrives. The leaves at the bottom fall first, and this might be due to fungal disease, drought, a lack of nutrients, or simply because it's fall and the plant is preparing for dormancy. Remove fallen leaves and keep the ground around the plant clean. Hopefully there are other plants between the roses that can hide some of the debris, nevertheless fallen leaves should be taken away since they can harbor and spread disease.

Continue irrigating the roses if it doesn't rain, but stop fertilizing them—they should not be fertilized in fall (which can begin at different times, depending on where you live in Sweden). This will encourage the plants to acclimatize to the upcoming winter cold, to stop growing, and to enter their dormant cycle.

Pile up soil around the rose canes to protect them against the winter cold.

Cover with leaves and fir branches for extra protection.

Cover

Once fall sets in for good there will be night frost, so it might be necessary to put a cover over the roses. Don't cover the plants too early, however, as this might do more harm than good. Wait until the first hard frost—the plants will have lost most of their leaves and they are now dormant.

Pile up plenty of dirt around the lower branches of bedding roses. If there isn't enough soil in the bed to do this (which is common), the soil may come from somewhere else: the vegetable patch, the compost pile, or from the beds of summer flowers.

Don't use peat moss or bark mulch to cover the roses—they both absorb water, which will later freeze into clumps of ice and choke the roses. Also, don't use commercial bagged soil, as it contains mostly peat moss and thus will absorb too much water. Add enough soil so that it makes a small hill around the bottom of the plant—make it approximately 15 to 20 cm (6" to 8") high from the top of the hill to the ground surface. If you plant your roses in the fall, add plenty of extra soil here too, and they'll survive the winter without any problems.

Winter cold

Winters have had a tendency to get milder in Sweden lately, the bitter cold not setting in until after the New Year. Snow provides a good cover for the roses; if there isn't any snow, however, you'll have to cover them with something else. You can use leaves in early winter, and then add fir branches on top or any other airy light material that will keep the leaves in place. Climbing roses set against a wall or a trellis can be protected with fir branches attached to the trellis, or by a woven grass mat, a shade cloth or some burlap hung in front.

The most difficult period for roses is typically in February and March when the spring sunshine is bright but the nights are still cold and the soil frozen. Don't be too hasty in uncovering the roses—leave it until spring has sprung for good.

Young shoots can be reddish in color and unexpectedly attractive.

Pruning roses

Most of the work that goes into growing roses is in the pruning. Individual roses are pruned according to their type, and while they're usually not killed by faulty pruning or even from non-pruning, the quality of the blooms might suffer. The time for pruning is in early spring, before the leaves start to appear. An old proverb says that the time is right when the birch leaves are big as mice ears. That size happens to be around 1 cm (.40"), and depending where you live it's roughly around April and May. Pruning can be done a bit earlier or later, but this is the general guideline.

Do not prune roses in the fall or winter—if you cut the branches and then go through a cold snap, the chill can penetrate through the cut. The roses will freeze, so you'll have to prune them again to get rid of the frozen parts. Special considerations for different types of roses are covered in different parts of this book, but all roses are pruned around the same time of the year. Let the size of the mouse's ear be your guide for all roses.

The root and the rose

Roses seldom grow from their own-root—at least not when purchased or when planted (see 'Roses in garden centers and in cultivation,' p. 136). This is why the root of another variety of rose can send up suckers that need to be quickly removed lest they overpower the grafted rose. Shoots from the root grow from the root ball down under the surface of the soil, not from the branches above the grafting spot (the grafting spot doesn't show if the rose is planted correctly). Shoots growing from the root are usually light green, long, thin, and grow much faster than the grafted rose. If you're unsure, wait until the plant starts to green out, then check the leaves. Root shoots have smaller leaves, and often many more sections per leaf. The canes are typically thornier and they grow like long antennas. It's best to cut them off all the way down by the root—pull at the sucker, move it back and forth, remove some of the soil from around it. Try to cut it about an inch below the surface to make it more difficult for it to re-grow; if it does reappear, the only thing is to remove it, again and again. In the fall, try digging up as much of the root as possible so you can cut off the root shoot altogether.

Bedding roses need to be pruned each year, but shrub roses and groundcover roses don't require it. An old proverb says that roses are to be pruned when 'the birch leaves are as big as mice ears'.

GENERAL RULES FOR PRUNING ROSES

- Prune off frozen, dead, broken, and damaged canes.
- Snip off faded leaves and flower debris.
- Even out taller canes or shoots with the rest of the plants.
- Remove root shoots from grafted roses (those not grown on their own-root)—see also 'Roses in Garden Centers and in Cultivation', p. 136.

A red bedding rose with flowering root shoot (suckers) from a Japanese climbing rose.

ROSES FOR THE FLOWERBED

The traditional place to grow roses is in the flowerbed, where they dazzle us as the colorful beauties they are.

So, which roses should you pick out for your garden? That's impossible to say, as it all depends on individual preferences, climate, location, and the way in which you plan to display them. The main difference between all types of good bedding roses lies in their size, color, and fragrance. "Good" in this case means healthy specimens with proven disease resistance, flowers that bloom easily and abundantly, and that are also easy to grow and care for. These aren't inherent qualities to all types of roses, and you will need time to assess them; you can't determine after only one year if a rose is healthy or not.

Height can vary as well, but that will depend on climate and pruning. Typically, bedding roses are 40 to 100 cm (15¾" to 39½") tall, with a few exceptions. All of them need sun, water, and nutrient-rich soil, so you can plant them together in the same area. You may choose to grow only a single type of rose or a combination of several specimens—either way they'll thrive together.

Large-flowered, small-flowered, single flowers or filled, double or half-double, short or tall—with roses, your options are diverse and plentiful. Single flowers are usually self-cleaning, as the faded petals drop to the ground themselves. Flowers that are richer in petals stay on the cane even when they're spent, so they need to be snipped off or deadheaded. Roses begin to flower as soon as the first year they're planted, so try out a few different ones. There are even container-grown flowering roses available for sale. Luckily, roses don't take up a lot of space so you can sample many varieties, and maybe even discover new favorites every year. Availability changes quickly, which makes it both necessary and possible to exchange old varieties for newer ones. Happily, almost all roses look wonderful together, regardless of color or shape.

Roses, either in single-type or multi-variety groupings, look beautiful in flowerbeds. Plant them close together to get luxuriant bunches of blooms. Their colors are usually very complementary.

Color and shape

Choosing among roses can offer up quite a challenge. There's such a vast array to pick from—around 13,000 specimens. Roses suitable for flowerbeds are collected under the generic term 'bedding roses,' but that is not a proper botanical group. Among the bedding roses you'll find floribundas, sprays, or polyanthas, which are essentially different names for nearly the same

thing—as well as large-flowered roses and many modern shrub roses. Large-flowered roses have one or two large elegant flowers per cane, like the well-known 'Peace' rose (*Rosa* Mme A. Meilland). Their other familiar appellation is hybrid tea roses, which look beautiful in a vase, and are what comes to mind when we think of cut roses sold commercially.

Sprays or polyantha roses produce more and smaller flowers in large sprays, but the distinction between large-flowered roses and polyanthas is not clear. Still, there is a discernible difference between the type of rose with a few really large blooms, and the types with more flowers. The two, however, are becoming more and more alike, which is why they're all grouped under the term bedding roses—a practical way to indicate their primary use. Modern shrub roses have a few more flowers in sprays—the flowers are a bit larger in smaller sprays, but even here you'll find variations among the types.

IMPORTANT CONSIDERATIONS WHEN CHOOSING A ROSE

- The quality of the specimen, or its hardiness and disease resistance.
- Hardiness (but proper soil and drainage are more important for overwintering).
- The size and growth habit—the final size of the plant.
- The type of flower—polyanthas, small-flowered or single large flowers.
- Flower color, shape and how it withers
- Fragrance
- Foliage color—dark red/green or light green, shiny or matte.

World's Favorite Roses

Below is a list of the world's most beloved roses, according to votes cast by the member countries of The World Federation of Rose Societies. The first year indicates the winning year; the second year tells us when the rose was launched, followed by the name of the breeder. Synonyms, when applicable, are shown within parentheses.

1976 'Peace' (syn. Gioia, Gloria dei, Mme. A. Meilland) 1945, France. Large-flowered, pale yellow.

1979 'Queen Elizabeth' 1954, Dr W.E. Lammerts, USA. Pure pink.

1981 'Fragrant Cloud' (syn. Duftwolke, Nuage Parfumé) 1963, Tantau, Germany. Large-flowered, red/pink.

1983 'Iceberg' (syn. Schneewittchen, Fée des Neiges) 1958, Kordes, Germany. Modern bush rose, white.

1985 'Double Delight' 1977, Herbert Swim, USA. Large-flowered, creamy white with cherry-pink outer rim.

1988 'Papa Meilland' 1963, Meilland, France. Large-flowered, dark red.

1991 'Pascali' (LENip) 1963, Louis Lens, Belgium. Large-flowered, white.

1994 'Just Joey' 1972, Roger Pawsey of Cants, England. Large-flowered, amber/copper.

1997 'New Dawn' 1930, a sport from Dr. W. Van Fleet, USA. Climber, light pink.

2000 'Ingrid Bergman' 1984, Olesen, Denmark. Large-flowered, red.

2003 'Bonica 82' (MEIdomonac) 1982, Meilland, France. Bush rose, groundcover, light pink.

2006 'Elina' (syn. Peaudouce) 1983, Dickson, Northern Ireland. Large-flowered, pale yellow/white.

2006 'Pierre de Ronsard' (syn. Eden, Eden Climber, Eden Rose 88, Grimpant de Pierre de Ronsard) 1987, Meilland, France. Large-flowered, very full pink, bowl shaped.

Many of these roses are popular and can be found on other top rose lists. In Sweden, the most popular specimens are still **'Nina Weibull'**, red; **'The Fairy'**, light pink; **'Friesia'**, yellow; **'Queen Elizabeth'**, pink; **'Peace'**, pale yellow, and the climbers **'New Dawn'**, light pink and **'Flammentanz'**, red/pink. All are old roses, and some—even though they're now of dubious quality—are still best sellers.

In 2006 'Peaudouce' was named 'the world's most beloved rose', a distinction bestowed by member rose societies all over the world. In spite of this, this particular rose has never achieved acclaim in Sweden, despite being available on the market since 1983.

Choosing roses for the flowerbed

Once you've decided where to plant your roses, you'll need to select the plants. Roses for beds are often chosen based on color and shape, since they have to fit in with other plants as well as with the house, the garage, or with a fence.

The roses here are grouped by color. Be aware that shades can vary depending on each person's perception of it—what might be red to you or me might look more like dark pink to someone else; white might seem pale yellow; the grades of orange/apricot are especially challenging to qualify. For each color grouping there are suggestions for large-flowered types and polyanthas. Some low-growing and some especially hardy specimens are also listed.

Selecting newer varieties

I, along with many other gardeners, feel that it's time to say goodbye to many of the old Swedish standard roses, as their disease resistance has declined substantially over the years, and roses with higher disease resistance are far easier to care for. The varieties featured in this book are a selection of the newer roses that can be found in well-stocked garden centers and plant nurseries. Naturally, not all shops will stock the full range of plants, but they can still all be found out there at various locations.

Hardiness is an important consideration in picking a rose if you live in a Swedish zone 3 or a colder climate. The hardiness zones are specific to the Riksförbundets Svensk Trädgård zone map for Sweden, an equivalent to the USDA hardiness zone map for the USA. While this map indicates the hardiness zone a garden is situated in, there might be some wiggle-room because soil quality and local climate still exert more influence than

A multi colored rose bed can occasionally remind us of a jar of pico de gallo salsa. As some plants die and new ones emerge, the effect is often much more eye-catching than one could hope for, so why pick only one rose to plant when you can enjoy many more?

a lot of people realize. A single garden can straddle three different hardiness zones depending on how protected or exposed the flowerbed is to the elements, which is why you should consider the zones listed here a guideline and not a hard and fast set of rules. The health of the rose depends more on the condition of the soil than on what type of rose it is, especially if the rose is to survive winter.

Most varieties are quite new—they've only been cultivated for a few years. If you spot a question mark after the zone listed by a rose, it means that it will hopefully survive in that area, but we're not entirely confident in that assessment at present. Don't take the zones as gospel, because even if a rose has been tested for over a decade, its

eleventh year might see it freeze and be its undoing. Avoid looking at roses as long-lived perennials; by all means swap them around for other varieties every few years.

Red roses

Truly deep, red, velvety roses are extremely popular, and the best sellers of them all are the polyanthas. Red roses can also be deep pink, red, or orange-red, which can be difficult to discern in a picture. When selecting red roses, it's especially important to check how they'll look once they've withered. Many intensely colored red roses quickly turn a purple-red, and later yet rose-lilac, once spent. This can be either beautiful or ugly, depending on the color

'Kensington', a newer true red bedding rose.

'Hope for Humanity' is very hardy.

of the freshly opened roses and other plants surrounding the faded roses. The leaf color can vary, too—there's a big difference between red-green foliage and vibrantly green leaves.

Many of us aim to grow roses commonly found in the industry, with a pointy bud and velvety deep red flower. In this category, the new large-flowered specimen called 'Isabella Rosselini' is an excellent choice—see p. 145. It resembles 'Ingrid Bergman' and is in fact considered to be its successor. The ever-popular 'Ingrid Bergman' has been on the market for twenty years now, and the time has come to replace it with a newer, fresher variety.

Large flowered roses

Name	Red roses	Swedish zone
'Barkarole'	large, full flower, black veined to dark red	3
'Black Baccara'	very beautiful, French; but not very hardy	1
'Burgundy'	large, full, dark blood-red flower	4
'Courage'	large and full dark red flower	4

Cluster-flowered roses

There are many fine red cluster-flowered roses, so there's no reason to settle for an older and weaker variety.

Name	Red roses	Swedish zone
'H. C. Andersen'	truly fine color with dark red/green leaves; quite disease resistant, a perfect bedding rose	4
'Kensington'	replacement for the fine but rather average 'Kronborg', from the Castle Collection, which now should be replaced with a newer variety with lighter green leaves	3-4
'Nadia Renaissance'	somewhat taller bush rose with full, dark red flowers and a slight fragrance	
'William Shakespeare 2000'	one of the few English red roses in a beautiful old rose variety; it veers more towards purple	2-3

Low-growing rose varieties

Name	Red roses	Swedish zone
'Golden Eye'	short, bushy, ground-covering new American variety with an open orange-red flower and a yellow eye.	4?
'Kordes Rose Rotila'	low-growing, healthy	3?
'Mystic Fairy'	an American variety of shrub rose with red double flowers	4?

Extra hardy

Name	Red roses	Swedish zone
'Hope for Humanity'	a Canadian variety with beautiful full double blooms	5?

'Sebastian Kneipp' mild

'Lion's-Rose'

The new 'Kronprinsesse Mary Castle' is yellow-white with fragrance. It was voted the most popular Danish rose by several public gardens.

White roses

White roses are gorgeous and simple to add to group plantings with other roses and plants. The bud might have a tinge of pink or yellow, but once opened the flower is white. The white is seldom pure, however—it often varies a little. There aren't quite as many standout white roses as there are pinks and reds, but breeders are hard at work producing more of them. White flowers have a tendency to develop brown spots from rain or garden pests.

Large flowered roses

The large-flowered white roses are very tempting to grow but they usually lack fragrance, which is a good excuse to try out newcomers on the market. None of the following are better than others.

Name	White roses	Swedish zone
'José Carreras'	mother-of-pearl white full flower with mild fragrance	3
'Karen Blixen'	beautiful pure white, but will nod if rained on	3
'Marvellous'	lime shifting to white, full flower with mild fragrance	3?
'Memoire'	creamy white, full flower with moderate fragrance	3?
'Monsoon'	full flower, shifting from creamy white to lime white	3
'Sebastian Kneipp'	white with yellow/pink center; myrrh, sweet fragrance	3?

Cluster-flowered roses

There are many interesting specimens here; several new German varieties look very promising in particular. 'Schneewitchen' is a very popular rose in Sweden, although in my experience this rose is vulnerable to disease. Others feel that it's more disease resistant. Good soil and placement are crucial to help it do well.

Name	White roses	Swedish zone
'Gråsten' ('Poulfeld')	a somewhat older Castle variety; available at most garden centers	3–4
'Katarina Zeimat'	a very old, low-growing rose; doesn't bloom continuously but is quite hardy; according to noted sources it survived winters during WWII while many other roses died	Possibly hardy in 5
'Kosmos'	a new German variety, apparently very healthy; old-fashioned shape with creamy white full flower; pay attention to spelling it with a 'K', as there is a French white rose named 'Cosmos' spelled with a 'C'	3?
'Ledreborg'	a newer white Castle rose	3–4
'Lion's-Rose'	somewhat new, charming cream shading to pink full flower, fragrant and apparently healthy	2–3?
'Winchester Cathedral'	perhaps the best of the English white roses	2–3

Low-growing roses

Name	White roses	Swedish zone
'Diamant'	good groundcover; German, new and untested	3?
'Little White Pet'	a dainty old rose with small pompom red buds; does not bloom continuously	3
'White Cover' ('Poulcov')	groundcover, suitable for companion planting and under taller roses. With adequate snow cover this rose is hardy in colder zones.	3–4

Extra hardy roses

Name	White roses	Swedish zone
'Morden Snowbeauty'	a low bedding rose and groundcover	5

'Marselisborg' with Swan River daisy   *'Goldmarie' is intensely yellow.*   *'Morden Sunrise'*

Yellow roses

Yellow is a very sought-after color, and there are many truly fine bedding roses within this range. Yellow roses can skew towards lime yellow and green, while darker varieties can lean towards orange and copper shades. It's difficult to provide an objective description of the colors of these roses. Do exercise caution when combining yellow roses with reds and pinks.

Yellow roses often have strong yellow/orange—almost red—buds. Unfortunately, in many varieties that bright color quickly fades to white once the flower has fully opened, and so can end up looking a bit dull. The extremely popular, and a best seller, 'Friesia' is such a rose, so there's no harm in replacing it with newer varieties that can hold their color longer. Yellow and pale pink roses can attract pollen beetles, but this is an issue that does not crop up every year.

Large-flowered roses

While most large-bloomed roses lack fragrance, some newer varieties have been bred to emit scent.

Name	Yellow roses	Swedish zone
'Glowing'	a new rose, pale yellow with mild fragrance	3?
'Kaj Munk'	average, full, pale yellow flower	3?
'Peaudouce' ('Elina')	an elegant, pale yellow rose that has existed since the 1980s without making its mark in Swedish gardens	3?
'Wonderful'	a new, pale yellow rose that is untested	3?

Cluster-flowered roses

These are commonly found in rose beds at the front of Swedish houses painted in the classical Falu oxblood color. There are many new fine varieties to try.

Name	Yellow roses	Swedish zone
'Crown Princess Margareta'	a very full English rose in amber and gold; not an overwhelming bloomer	2–3
'Golden Celebration'	a warm yellow English rose that retains its color well	2–3
'Goldmarie'	a luminous yellow rose that withers nicely without fading	3–4
'Graham Thomas'	a fine, warm yellow English rose	2–3
'Gripsholm'	a lighter yellow castle rose that is a productive bloomer; easy to find in Swedish garden centers	3–4
'Macy's Pride'	a soft yellow to creamy white rose; new, American, and untested	4?
'Marselisborg'	a soft yellow castle rose that turns slightly pink when withered	4
'Sophia Renaissance'	a soft, warm yellow full flower that fades to chamois yellow; mild fragrance	3–4

Low-growing roses

Name	Yellow roses	Swedish zone
'Golden Eye Cover'	a groundcover that looks promising; small, semi-double flower	4
'Olympic Palace'	low-growing with a warm yellow flower; can be used as container rose	3?

Extra hardy

Name	Yellow roses	Swedish zone
'Morden Sunrise'	semi-double, fully open flower; color shifts to copper toward the petal's edge	4–5?

'Westerland' is surprisingly hardy.

'Flora Danica' has a faint fragrance.

'Trelleborg'—color changes depending on the weather.

Apricot, copper yellow, and orange roses

Apricot, copper yellow, and orange roses have become incredibly popular. The color is quite new; very few old roses can be found in these particular shades. Colors can shift a lot depending on the plant's location as well as its age. The flower can open in pink-apricot then darken to orange, or open in orange and lighten to pink. Some rose varieties are bred to turn, as they mature, from yellow to orange to copper red. In general, orange roses also change color according to temperature and weather, so a bed full of orange roses can therefore appear different from one year to the next, making it hard to predict the end result.

Large-flowered roses

Name	Apricot, copper yellow & orange roses	Swedish zone
'Alexander'	an older orange-red variety; quite hardy	4–5
'Dronning Ingrid'	an intense orange-red sport of 'Flora Danica'	3–4?
'Flora Danica'	orange with yellow tone, sturdy with dark foliage and a hint of fragrance	4?

Cluster-flowered roses

These can shift in color even more. As a cluster, withered flowers stay bunched together with buds and opening flowers, making these roses' appearance change from day to day.

Name	Apricot, copper yellow & orange roses	Swedish zone
'Aprikola'	a promising new, very healthy German rose; apricot color with some fragrance (p. 36, 42)	3?
'Celebration'	an English rose in an unusual pink/orange shade	2–3
'Gebrüder Grimm'	an interesting new bi-colored rose, very popular in Germany; belongs to the Märchenrosen series; pinkish red interior with yellow-orange exterior	3?
'Kalmar'	a much-liked apricot Castle rose; very popular in England under another name	3–4
'Sangerhausen Jubilee'	full flower in shades ranging from apricot orange to pink; some fragrance; belongs to the Märchenrosen series	3?
'Trelleborg'	an incredibly beautiful Castle rose in shifting apricot-pink-orange shades	3–4
'Westerland'	belongs to the best and hardiest of this group; shifts greatly in color	5

Low-growing roses

Name	Apricot, copper yellow & orange roses	Swedish zone
'Flaming Cover'	a newer variety with small golden yellow and orange flowers with a hint of copper	3–4

Extra hardy roses

Name	Apricot, copper yellow & orange roses	Swedish zone
'Morden Fireglow'	more fire red than orange	4–5?

'Paul McCartney' is only slightly scented.

Pink roses

Pink is arguably the most common color for roses. Wild (species) roses are typically pink, and there are many pink roses that are hardy and disease resistant. The color can shift from near white to blush, to intense cherry, to near red. Pink can also have blue undertones in it, with a hint of violet or yellow moving it towards salmon pink and apricot. Pink-toned roses change when withered, and can become either darker or lighter in color. Light pink varieties usually turn pale in strong sunshine, and can get speckled with brown spots in rainy weather.

Large-flowered roses

Name	Pink roses	Swedish zone
'Extravaganza'	full flower; light apricot	3?
'Louisiana'	dark pink with good fragrance	4 (maybe)
'Majestic'	pale pink with some apricot; hint of fragrance	3
'Paul McCartney'	strong pink and surprisingly fragrant for a large-flowered rose	3
'Royal Copenhagen'	hint of pink in almost white full flower	3
'Scented Memory'	apricot shifting to pink	3?
'Sentimental'	dark pink to pink red	3?

Cluster-flowered roses

Cluster-flowered pink roses are almost as popular as their red counterparts. The bestseller is the low-growing 'The Fairy', which is now 75 years old. Also popular is 'Sommerwind' in the same shade of baby pink, featuring a larger flower. There is an incredible amount of new, fine varieties both in salmon pink, pale pink and cherry, which adds a bit of diversity in the rose bed.

Name	Pink roses	Swedish zone
'Astrid Lindgren'	A favorite of many (not one of mine, however); light pink flower and upright sturdy growth	4
'Avila'	a new, intense dark pink Castle rose	3-4
'Berleburg'	a very full, cherry-pink Castle rose	3-4
'Carcassonne'	a newer, light pink Castle rose; untried	3-4
'Clair Renaissance'	one of the more popular newer roses; very pale pink	3-4
'Home & Garden'	a nostalgic rose with full pink flower; a healthy variety from Kordes' Märchenrosen series	3-4?
'Leonardo da Vinci'	a popular rose with beautifully full dark pink flowers; French Romantica series; its hardiness is questionable	3?
'Maria Renaissance'	a new variety with a beautiful full cherry-pink flower	3-4
'Maxi Vita'	a flower with a hint of salmon in the pink; a healthy new variety in Kordes' Rigo Rosen series	3-4?
'Neon'	a bright pink flower; a healthy variety from Kordes' Rigo Rosen series	3-4?
'Noble Anthony'	one of the better dark pink English varieties	2-3
'Queen of Sweden'	a newer English rose in delicate porcelain pink	2-3
'Pomponella'	a beautiful small cherry-pink candy-like flower globe; a healthy variety from Kordes' Märchenrosen series	3-4
'Poulsen's Pearl'	an old variety that has regained popularity; unique single flower	4 (maybe)
'Romanze'	an attractive cherry pink semi-double flower with a scalloped edge and dark green glossy foliage	4
'Rosenfess'	light pink with a hint of apricot; a healthy new variety in Kordes' Märchenrosen series	3-4
'Sommer 2000'	a dark pink version of 'Sommerwind'	4
'Wisby'	a new Castle rose; full and light pink	3-4

Low-growing roses

Name	Pink roses	Swedish zone
'Little Mischief'	an American, small, full, low-growing cherry-colored flower	4?
'Sommerwind'	baby pink, low growing, very useful and easily cultivated	4–5
'The Fairy'	both hardy and forgiving	5

Extra hardy

Name	Pink roses	Swedish zone
'Morden Blush'	light pink	5
'Morden Centennial'	pink	5
'Morden Ruby'	often called red but is in fact deep pink. If planted with bright red roses the color difference emerges	5

Salmon pink varieties

Salmon pink is an intense and unique color that can often be challenging to match with other pinks. However, in the right company this color provides a good transition from apricot-orange varieties to pink tones within the same rose bed.

Name	Salmon pink roses	Swedish zone
'Amelia Renaissance'	full, assertive salmon pink, some fragrance	3–4
'Anna'	a Swedish variety with attractive and shifting color, well worth a try; flowers on young plant, and can grow into a shrub; see 'Roses as shrubs,' p. 74	3?
'Bonita Renaissance'	salmon orange	3–4
'Glamour'	large-flowered salmon pink with mild fragrance	3
'Läckö'	a vibrantly colored Castle rose known in Denmark by the name 'Riberhus'; a prolific bloomer that's quite easily found in Scandinavian garden centers	3–4

'Home & Garden' is a healthy variety.

'Queen of Sweden' is a newer English variety.

'Leonardo da Vinci' has been voted Sweden's most beautiful rose.

'Wisby' is named after Visby Castle, Sweden.

'Läckö' , a Castle rose and prolific bloomer.

'Morden Ruby' is hardy.

Blue, purple, and violet roses

Blue is—and has been for many years—the color of roses that breeders dream of and aspire to capture. A bright blue rose has yet to see the light of day—advertising spreads featuring photos of blue roses have been airbrushed and color-manipulated, since these flowers cannot be found in nature. The quest for a true blue rose has brought about varieties of violet-hued flowers of inferior quality, which have been making their appearance on the market. The best specimen so far is 'Rhapsody in Blue', which features blue-violet flowers that are reminiscent of the Japanese rose. It has quickly become in demand.

The violet color changes with the weather. In cool temperatures, the color can look deeply purple, while in a heat wave it can become a bleached pale pink. The flowers usually turn slightly grey with silver notes when they wither.

'Rhapsody in Blue' and the light 'Bering Renaissance'.

Cluster-flowered roses

Exist in both darker and lighter shades

Name	Blue, purple and violet roses	Swedish zone
'Bering Renaissance'	delightful light lilac color; fragrant	3–4
'Lambert'	a newer Castle rose in coveted color	3–4
'Rhapsody in Blue'	a sturdy and firm plant; dark red purple	3–4
'Sandra Renaissance'	more pink than purple, also called lavender pink; some fragrance	3?

Large-flowered roses

Typically very pale violet in color.

Name	Blue, purple and violet roses	Swedish zone
'Oiseau Bleu'	very popular purple to violet pink; some fragrance	2–3?
'Stunning'	lavender pink to violet pink, some fragrance	3?
'The Scotsman'	lavender pink; is blemished by rain	3?

Dream roses

Multicolored roses have been popular for several centuries. Here too, inferior plants are being introduced on the market simply because their striping is so attractive. Pink-white striping already exists in nature, so what's being sought after are yellow-orange striping as well as other atypical or rare combinations. One series of striped roses is called 'Rose des Peintres' (the painters' rose), which includes roses named after famous artists. However, even breeders will admit that these are not the best specimens. But they're still very popular with customers because their colors are so pretty. Their hardiness is dubious, and the varieties can 'revert' back to type—i.e. all the flowers don't turn out striped.

The striping also varies depending on the age of the plant, the weather, and whether it's the beginning or end of summer. New striped roses appear all the time but vanish just as quickly, so it's not easy to recommend a specific plant. One good striped variety with a low-growing habit that's suitable for a rose bed, an edging, or front-row shrubs, is 'Candy Cover' in pink, red, and white, zone 3–4.

Bi-colored roses can feature one color in the middle and be bordered by another. Some varieties have a darker edge on each petal, and they're more reliable color-wise than their striped counterparts. There aren't that many out there, but some of them are truly lovely plants.

Next two pages: 'Aprikola'.

Multi colored roses

Name	Multi colored roses	Swedish zone
'Love and Peace'	Prize-winning cross with 'Peace'. A new American variety which has sparked some interest. Warm yellow with dark pink edges and red outer petals. Not available in Sweden as of yet.	3?
'Nostalgie'	a large-flowering white rose with red edging. Very impressive, but it can be a long wait between blooms; see p. 39 for picture.	3
'Peace'	a well-known bi-colored rose; will vary in how much pink and yellow each flower exhibits. Occasionally gives the impression of having only a single color.	2–3
'Rose Gaujard'	an older favorite; silver white with a pink-red edge; a crossbreed with 'Peace' as the parent plant.	2–3

Mix it up—find delight in the old and the new

Roses are beautiful flowers and most roses go well together. Mix and match them to your heart's content—small flowering varieties with large-blooms own-root roses; red with pink, yellow, and orange. All roses require a sunny spot with good, loose soil, plenty of water and nutrients in order to thrive, to look and to show their best. If the roses are healthy their care will be easy, including snipping and deadheading. Pruning time is in the spring.

POM

You should not remove very old rose bushes before you've made sure that they're not rare specimens; they could be a unique plant that is no longer commercially available. Old shrub roses with an authenticated age of at least 50 years are of great interest. In Sweden, for more information go to POM, (Programmet för Odlad Mångfald—The Program for Diversity of Cultivated Plants: www.pom.info; you can also inquire by email: gamlarosor@pom.info

Pruning bedding roses

Bedding roses get pruned the hardest. The canes are cut about 10–20 cm (4" to 8") above the soil surface, leaving about five to six bud eyes (the eyes look like a tiny pins in the bark). The purpose of pruning is to get low-growing, profusely flowering roses. The height of a rose given in catalogues refers to a rose that is pruned yearly. If the canes aren't pruned near the ground, they will continue to grow and the plant becomes higher each year. It won't die, but it will become very straggly. A five-foot 'Peace' rose isn't the mark of a superior cultivator, but a sign that the plant has not been pruned.

You can let roses grow a little taller next to a house or at the back of a rose bed, if you like. Otherwise, the general recommendation is to prune hard, so that the plant can produce many new side shoots, which is where new flowers will bloom. Old, neglected, or un-pruned plants produce few new shoots and flowers.

Pruning of bedding roses in cold climates

Rose canes often freeze in colder areas of Sweden, so you'll have to prune the cane right under the frozen part. You'll notice the difference: the frozen part of the cane is dark brown or deep red, dry, or a shriveled light brown, whereas the healthy part is green or reddish green, depending on plant variety. If you're unsure, carefully scrape the surface of the cane with a fingernail—it will show through white and light green if it's healthy. But it doesn't matter what kind of rose it is—if the cane is dead, snip it off.

Unpruned 'Peace' roses can reach many feet in height.

A standard (tree) rose is pruned like a bedding rose.

A few long stragglers showing above the other canes need to be pruned.

If the plant has sprouted many small, thin, and short shoots, snip them off. Save only five to seven of the strongest shoots evenly distributed around the plant, and remove the unnecessary shoots and the suckers. The small shoots are of no benefit to the plant since they will never become flowering canes. The older the plant, the coarser the main trunk the canes grow from. Do not cut or saw the main trunk. When roses get old and their trunk only produces a couple of canes, it might be time to replace the rose.

Tree roses are rose plants trained to grow in trunk height. They're pruned the same way as bedding roses, i.e. leaving canes with five to six bud eyes. Don't touch the brown bud union in the middle—just the canes growing out from it. Remove the thin, straggly shoots and save the strong shoots that are evenly distributed around the plant.

Pruning bedding roses in the summer

We like to see our rose bushes grow evenly and attractively. If one shoot is much longer than the rest, just trim it. If you don't, it will continue to grow at the expense of smaller shoots, which in turn will end up lagging behind.

Roses vary in the way they grow. Some, like 'Nostalgie', willingly send up a few strong shoots, while others grow more evenly on their own.

Trivia for the rose enthusiast

As you look at roses in catalogs, on lists of favorites, and in garden centers, you can quickly find yourself buried in an avalanche of information. Without wading too deeply into the topic, I'll sort through and clarify some of it here.

Rose breeders launch new roses every year. Mogens Olesen, from the Danish firm Poulsen's, is the breeder located furthest north in Scandinavia. Poulsen's varieties have always been popular in Sweden, since roses bred for the Danish climate are most likely hardier than roses bred for German or French environments.

Currently, breeders launch their roses in product batches or series. New roses are called by standardized names and put into groups; roses within a group can, however, still be pretty distinctive from one another. They don't need to be of the same lineage to end up in the same product group. Furthermore, just because one or two specimens in a group prove to be inferior doesn't necessarily mean that all the plants in that particular group are subpar.

Old-fashioned English charm

The group or series called Austin Roses—also referred to as English Roses—combines old-world charm and looks with modern colors and longer lasting blooms; they're a collection of modern shrub roses bred by David Austin. An old rose and a modern rose were used at the onset to reproduce the fragrance and shape of ancient roses in newer varieties. He continued the hybridization of his own breeds with other varieties, which imparts today's English roses with as mixed a background as any other modern rose.

Austin roses are sold in special containers and the license tax is higher than on other roses, so these flowers end up being a bit more expensive. They hardly ever attain full shrub size in our climate, but a few examples can grow quite large and handsome. Some varieties are hardier than others, but many develop nodding flowers like many other old-world roses. Some varieties' flowers are so full that instead of opening fully, they rot, while others flower only sparingly. Their hardiness is a little uneven (possibly Swedish zone 2–3) and they are not suitable for planting further up north unless they're grown in containers.

Below are some suggestions for some of the best English roses and their different colors. There are many varieties, including three to five new roses launched each year, and availability changes quickly.

'Abraham Darby', soft pink.
'Celebration', salmon pink.
'Charles Austin', yellow.
'Constance Spry', the very first David Austin rose; pink.
'Crown Princess Margareta', copper yellow.
'Emanuel', mild yellow white, to white.
'Golden Celebration', yellow.
'Graham Thomas', yellow.
'Lady Filippa Hamilton', orange red with dark foliage.
'Queen of Sweden', new, beautifully light pink.
'William Shakespeare 2000', dark red.
'Winchester Cathedral', white.

'Crown Princess Margareta' is a well-known David Austin rose.

'Lea Renaissance' is very similar to an old-fashioned shrub rose.

Danish charmer 'Nadia Renaissance'.

Several different English roses, en masse (mass planting).

A major Danish rose company

The Danish company Poulsen's also invests in old-fashioned yet modern roses with fragrance. One series is called Renaissance roses, and these flowers are probably a bit hardier—Swedish zone 3–4—than English roses. They can grow quite tall and sturdy, and can be found in all colors and in very fine specimens. They all have girls' names, followed by the word 'Renaissance.'

A bit further down the line is a group labeled Castle roses, which first were named after Danish castles such as 'Gråsten'. Nowadays, however, there are so many varieties in this group that there aren't enough Danish castles left to provide them all with names; French and English castles such as 'Limoges' and 'Kensington' have thus been called upon to help brand the newer varieties.

Poulsen's is also launching the series called Cover roses, which are low-growing, prolific bloomers suitable for under planting with the Castle roses. All varieties have names followed by 'Cover.' They still continue to develop stylish large-flowered roses; the series named paramount, for example, features very large blooms in modern shades, and some emit fragrance. Nevertheless, lately they seem to be putting more emphasis on producing compact flowers.

In 1939, the RNRS (Royal National Rose Society) arranged for an election to be held among professionals and amateurs to find out what they considered to be the best roses. The winning varieties were 'Else Poulsen', 'Anne Mette Poulsen', 'Karen Poulsen', 'Kirsten Poulsen', 'Betty Prior', and 'Donald Prior'. Four winning roses from Poulsen's demonstrates the influence the company exerted in the field, and still does to this day. Because of this, it's a pleasure to be able to show some examples of their newer varieties in this book.

Fragrant romance

Even the great and venerable French company Meilland is working along the same lines as Austin and Poulsen's to produce old-fashioned fragrance and color in new varieties of roses. Their series of old-world roses is called Romantica, and 'Leonardo da Vinci', which was voted Sweden's most beautiful rose by Trädgårdsföreningen (The Garden Society) in Gothenburg, Sweden, is one of the standouts in that series. 'Paul McCartney' is a large-flowered dark pink modern rose with old-fashioned fragrance; it's very rare that large-bloomed roses emit such pronounced fragrance. Parfums de Provence is another series of fragrant roses, but the hardiness of its varieties is up for debate. Their series also comprise many fine groundcover roses, where 'Bonica' is the most well known, and 'Swany' is one of the most common of the white roses.

Vibrant color, health, and disease resistance

The German company Kordes operates more on tradition—they launch strong varieties in bright colors like 'Goldmarie', but sadly the plants often lack fragrance. Recently they've been concentrating on rose health, which is now becoming evident in their offerings. These roses can be a bit difficult to get a hold of, but they're available through special order; several of their newer varieties will most likely be introduced in Sweden in the near future.

Märchenrosen—fairytale roses—are the equivalent of English roses, usually in clusters of charmingly fragrant and full flowers. Hardiness might be a Swedish zone 3 but can be stronger—this will prove itself in time. Many older Kordes roses have proven to be very hardy.

'Cinderella', pale pink.
'Gebrüder Grimm', orange and reddish pink.
'Home & Garden', beautiful pink; not quite a new variety.
'Kosmos', deliciously creamy white, quite tall, healthy; with some fragrance.
'Pomponella', dark pink, marzipan confectionery-style rose.
'Sangerhausen Jubilee', full pale apricot/orange-pink flower.
'Rigo Rosen' is a series of especially hardy and disease resistant varieties; not yet tested but probably a Swedish zone 3-4.
'Aprikola', apricot orange.
'Bad Birnach', low, pink, cupped, pointy bloom.
'Diamant', low-growing, white.
'Fortuna', low-growing, simple pink flower.
'Gärtnerfreude', low-growing, pink red
'Innocencia', low-growing, white.
'Kordes Rose Rotila', red and very healthy
'Maxi Vita', pink with a hint of salmon.
'Neon', cherry pink.

'Aprikola', a rose from the German company Kordes.

New American own-root varieties

Bailey Nurseries is an American garden nursery that started its own rose breeding operation in 1991. They focus on own-root, disease resistant, and hardy roses. The concept behind Easy Elegance roses emphasizes that these flowers are easy to care for and will bloom continuously through the season. Bailey's also feature several series; still, it's best to choose the rose according to the individual variety's properties. Hardiness is set at Swedish zone 4 but they have survived the test of two winters in Swedish zone 5, which is too short a timeframe to draw any definitive conclusions. At the moment there are only a few specimens available on the Swedish market, but more are sure to follow if these initial roses perform well.

The series Garden Jubilee are shrub roses with bi-colored flowers.
'Funny Face', white and pink painted flowers.
'Golden Eye', red with yellow eye.
The Garden Path series have low-growing groundcovers; used to edge garden paths.
'Little Mischief', semi-double red with white eye.
'Mystic Fairy', reddish pink like 'The Fairy'.
The Garden Art series combines traditional large-flowered blooms with a shrub rose toughness; hardiness is perhaps up to Swedish zone 3–4?
'Macy's Pride', a creamy yellow.
Hardiest and easiest to care for are the roses included in the Lifestyle Garden series.
The white 'Snowdrift' and red 'My Hero'—both being test-grown.

'Golden Eye' is an American variety.

Canadian roses—the tough and hardy guys amongst the bedding roses

'Canadian' here means having been bred in Canada—it is not its own discrete group of roses. The common denominator is that these varieties are bred to be hardy in Canada's rough climate of severe winter cold, snow, and short, warm summers. This doesn't necessarily mean that they will take easily to Swedish winters, where temperatures can fluctuate wildly and the snow does melt at times.

There are several different series or product groups, like Explorer and Parkland for instance, which are looked at in closer detail in the section called 'Roses as shrubs,' p. 74. Many of the Canadian roses are low growing and make good bedding roses, especially the Morden varieties. These are not at all suitable for the south of Sweden, however, as they can succumb to diseases that would otherwise not affect them in colder climates.

Rose names in modern times

Scientific names were given to old roses many years ago, and referred to the wild species roses they originated from. Modern-day roses, on the other hand, have other sorts of names, since they've been hybridized to such an extent that it's difficult to establish what they truly are. Many varieties are named after people, places or events—some varieties even answer to several names.

A modern rose like 'Ingrid Bergman' is written *Rosa* 'Ingrid Bergman', which is the plant's commercial name. However, modern roses' most important identifier is their code name, or registration name, which lets the breeder know who owns the patent on the breed. This is usually indicated by the first three to four letters (in capitals) and the rest is in lower case,

which varies and is unique for each variety. The code/registration name always begins with the breeder's specific abbreviation; the code name for 'Ingrid Bergman' is POULman. This name is unique and can never be changed. POUL tells us that this is a Poulsen rose, while the rest of the letters stand for 'Ingrid Bergman's unique ID.

The code name is of no interest to us customers; instead, we refer to the 'shop' name, as it were. The marketing name for a single rose can also vary from country to country, because names are directly linked to sales; names that are popular in the breeder's homeland don't necessarily translate or sell well in other countries. For example, Denmark sells a rose called 'Gavnø'; the same rose is sold in England as 'Buck's Fizz', named

after the musical group that won the Eurovision Song Contest in 1981. The code/registration name for 'Gavnø' is POULgav.

The Castle rose 'Kalmar' is also named 'Apricot Castle' and 'Lazy Days', but use the code name POULkalm if you want to be absolutely certain you're getting the correct rose. Many roses also go by their original names translated into different languages; the German 'Sommerwind', for example, turns into 'Summerwind' in England. It's common to have English, French, and German translations of names tossed about between countries, but this can definitely give rise to some degrees of confusion. Misspellings and misunderstandings, however, can also give birth to 'new' names.

ROSES AS A GROUND-COVER

Roses can be used in landscapes in several ways, one of which is groundcover. We call varieties with long canes and spreading growth habits 'groundcovers,' because their principal trait is that they're much wider than they are tall. Some can reach over a meter high (3') and spread, while others hug the ground. The extent of the coverage will depend on the variety's growth habit, so it's best to select a flower to suit its growth site.

Different types of roses can be used as groundcover. There isn't one specific variety of rose that's used as groundcover above all others, and roses with spreading growth habits aren't closer to each other botanically than to any other rose—it's merely a practical moniker, since roses are sorted according to growth habit. Low growing varieties are selected to edge flowerbeds mostly, or to plant under taller, upright roses. Varieties that spread wide and have a tight-knit growth work well on slopes. The most vigorous growers with long and lanky canes typically feature small simple flowers with copious—if not continuous—blooms. On the other hand, full, large-flowered specimens are lower to the ground and have a less vigorous growth habit. The general rule of thumb is: the more impressive the flower, the smaller the plant, and the more challenging it is to care for.

'Viking' in the company of Lamb's Ears and the roses 'Anna' and 'Ritausma'.

A single plant of 'Flower Carpet', and still it covers one meter (3'). Here seen in the company of other groundcover roses like 'Snow Cover', 'Fairy Dance' and 'Mystic Fairy'.

Choosing groundcover roses

Groundcover roses are a relatively new concept; due to today's preference for easy-care yards over high-maintenance gardens, demand for this type of flower has grown steadily, and more varieties have been developed and launched. Naturally, choice of shapes and sizes within this category is somewhat limited as of yet, as there are nowhere near as many offerings in groundcover roses as in the more upright, classic bedding roses. Color options are limited, too—the most vigorous growers tend to be pink.

A few varieties are sufficient as long as they grow reasonably well, are resilient, and disease resistant. This latter point is very important, because groundcover roses don't get pruned often, which means that any overwintering pests that have latched onto the canes do not get cut away. It's better not to clean inside the mass of tangled rose canes and to leave all the old fallen leaves where they are; if they happen to be infected by a fungal disease or pest, disturbing the leaves and canes might spread the infection or infestation to the rest of the plant. Disease resistance is of utmost importance if you want to grow low maintenance groundcover roses. In most cases pink and white specimens are the most hardy and disease-resistant types, but there are, of course, exceptions to the rule.

Newly planted 'Flower Carpet' in June.

Flowering 'Flower Carpet' later that same summer.

'Sommerwind' is the same color as 'The Fairy', but its petals are larger and have picoted edges.

'White Cover' typifies a popular rose that is known under several different names. Registration or code name is POULcov; synonyms are: 'Kent', 'Latina', 'Pyrénées' and 'Sparkling White'.

Common groundcover roses

Name	Description	Swedish zone
'Alba Meidiland'	white, vigorous grower, small flower	3–4
'Bonica'	light pink, vigorous grower	4–5
'Flower Carpet' (also known as 'Heidetraum')	cherry pink, double small flower, very disease resistant and vigorous	4–5
'Fru Dagmar Kastrup'	Species rose, simple rose hip flower, gives hips	6
'Pink Meidiland'	simple, reddish pink with white eye	3
'Sommermärchen' (also known as 'Berkshire')	cherry pink, newer variety	3–4
'Sommerwind' (also known as 'Surrey')	light pink, same color as 'The Fairy' but its petals are larger with picoted edges	4
'Swany'	small, cupped white flower; very glossy green leaves	3–4
'The Fairy'	popular, baby pink, slightly late bloomer	5
'Fairy Dance'	red version of 'The Fairy'	4
'Lovely Fairy'	distinctly darker pink flower than 'The Fairy'; quite common	4
'Yellow Fairy'	yellow flower; not as good or vigorous a grower as the original rose	3–4
'Tommelise' (also known as 'Hertfordshire', Sandefjord')	simple, pinkish red small flower with yellow eye; vigorous grower	4
'Viking' (also known as 'Rody')	red-pink flower; interesting variety	4
'White Cover'	white; one of the best	4

The well-known rose called 'The Fairy', together with an unknown rose—most likely 'Swany'. There isn't a lot of variety in groundcovers available at garden centers; these roses were planted about ten years ago, when there were even fewer to pick from.

Popular varieties

Before choosing your roses, it's always good to see them up close and in situ. It's easier than you'd think when it comes to groundcover roses. 'The Fairy' dominates the market completely—if you notice groundcover roses used as bedding roses in Swedish municipal parks or other public places, chances are you're looking at 'The Fairy'. Originating in the 1930s, it became very popular in the 1980s and sales are still going strong today. Popular varieties are often copied, so there are several different versions of 'The Fairy'. They all look very much alike, although they come in different shades.

'Bonica' is a common groundcover rose. Its flowers are larger than 'The Fairy's, but their color is identical. It can grow to about one meter (3') in height, and is a prolific bloomer. 'Bonica', like 'The Fairy', is often found in public gardens throughout Sweden, England and France. 'Alba Meidiland' is quite large, with white flowers. It can grow up to one meter (3') high, has soft canes that bend out, and is very popular because of its mass showing of flowers. All three rose varieties are getting on a bit in age, however, so we should be seeing improvements in their updated counterparts.

'Flower Carpet' is a healthy and vigorous grower that has become a best seller in, among other places, the United States, where it's marketed as an eco-friendly rose and is sold in pink containers. It hasn't really wowed the Swedes yet, but it's nevertheless incredibly prolific and disease resistant. When other roses show black spots on their foliage, this one stays green and healthy, and grows vigorously. It's one of my favorites, and I recommend it enthusiastically.

Groundcover roses

Danish varieties of roses currently arouse the most interest in Sweden, but so do some new German, American and Canadian specimens. French types are less hardy, but a few, such as 'Swany' and 'Bonica', are surprisingly hardy and will probably do well in snowy locations. Many low growing roses that make acceptable groundcovers are mentioned in 'Roses for the flowerbed'—see p. 24. The varieties listed here, however, make distinctly better groundcovers. Since they are not a discrete group in their own right, they can usually be found among the selection of bedding roses at garden centers.

Unfortunately, the nomenclature of roses, confusing as it can be for the flowers as a whole, is even more baffling when it comes to groundcover roses. The selection is the same throughout Europe without any significant deviations, but the roses are sold under an array of names, some of which you'll encounter in this text.

'Linnaeus' is a new, rather tall, groundcover rose in exciting color.

New varieties of groundcover roses

Unfortunately, you won't find dependable, well performing groundcover roses in many of the colors that you see in bedding roses. New varieties are launched regularly, but not at anywhere near the same rate as bedding roses. It's a question of trial and error; also, the orange and dark red varieties tend to be uneven in quality. The biggest selection comes from the Danish company Poulsen, and the German outfit Kordes. Both breeders emphasize the development of healthy and hardy roses well suited to grow in public gardens and spaces. The American company Bailey Nurseries offers a series of low shrub roses called Garden Path. Even the Canadian series contains several groundcover varieties such as 'Morden Snowbeauty'—see 'Roses as shrubs,' p. 74.

Vigorous growers

Danish cottage roses are worth trying out if you have large areas to cover. Reminiscent of farm cottage roses, they're a new variety of garden and landscaping rose. 'Linnaeus' is available at garden centers, and its colors are bright yellow and orange in a single to semi-double flower. The advantage of single flowers is that they're self-cleaning—no snipping and deadheading is needed to prompt new flowers to bloom. Growers demonstrate this by tapping on the flowering plant with a stick, to show that all withered petals fall to the ground. The plant also has a cleaner, fresher look when there are no withered petals attached to it.

The flowers are small—they're only about an inch in diameter. All varieties produce attractive hips in the fall, and they're probably hardy to Swedish zones 4 or higher. Four plants will cover 1 m² (10 sq ft) and reach about 1 meter (3 ft) in height. Mature plants only need a slight top cut, if at all. They can be used as groundcover, in mass plantings or as low hedges.

Edging for the flowerbed

There are also newer varieties with less sturdy growth that feature full or double flowers. Danish, German and French types are being introduced, but not many of them are available yet at Swedish garden centers. The expansive Danish series with 'Cover' in the name includes a few different types of roses; some are lower growing with a more compact shape, while others sprawl out a bit more. The series features many shades, and the flowers are hardy up to Swedish zones 3–4. These varieties are sold in England and in the US under different names; some of them are almost twenty years old, but new and improved specimens are being introduced all the time.

Farm cottage roses in two colors, 'Linnaeus' and reddish pink 'Marsh'.

Several types of low groundcover roses surrounded by lamb's ears; 'Pink Cover' is at the front.

Smaller groundcover roses

Name	Description	Height
'Bayernland Cover'	small, semi-double, dark pink; prize-winner	60–100 cm (24" to 40")
'Bright Cover'	a large-flowering white rose with red edging; very impressive, but it can be a long wait between blooms—see p. 39 for picture	60–100 cm (24" to 40")
'Candy Cover'	semi-double, stripy red/white	60–80 cm (24" to 32")
'Cherry Cover'	small, semi-double, pinkish red	60–80 cm (24" to 32")
'Dawn Cover'	new medium red, single small flower, small	40–60 cm (14" to 24")
'Easy Cover'	small, double, light pink	40–60 cm (14" to 24")
'Flaming Cover'	new; yellow orange, semi-double; sets hips	40–60 cm (14" to 24")
'Gentle Cover'	small, semi-double, light pink; prize winner	30–50 cm (12" to 20")
'Golden Eye Cover'	new, semi-double yellow with darker eye; sets hips	40–60 cm (14" to 24")
'Intense Cover'	dark red, semi-double	60–80 cm (24" to 32")
'Pink Cover'	very small, single dark pink, from seed from 'The Fairy'	80–100 cm (32" to 40")
'Soft Cover'	pink to dark pink, semi-double very small flower	40–60 cm (14" to 24")

Planting on slopes and in beds

Groundcover roses are both beautiful and easy to care for when they're planted on slopes. No mowing and weeding is required, and you'll still see an abundance of glorious flowers over the whole summer. Groundcover roses need not—indeed, should not—be pruned. Their only requirement is to plant them in weed-free soil and to select vigorously growing varieties.

Roses are very thorny plants, so it can be a challenge to weed between the spreading, prickly canes of groundcover roses. To avoid this, some specific prep work is in order before you plant this type of groundcover. Roses will cover the ground and prevent weeds from emerging, but they need some help in their first year, before the plant has become established and has had time to develop. All soil contains weed seeds—even soil bought by the truckload—so you'll need to remove all weeds before planting these roses in the soil. If you plant several groundcover roses, you should cover the soil before planting in it to avoid having to weed later on. See detailed description in 'Roses the easy way,' p. 91.

By all means, plant your roses closer together than recommended; standard instructions are typically meant only for public gardens. If you plant them snugly, the area will look nicer a lot faster, and the ground will be covered more quickly. In fact, it's not a bad idea to put in more plants in order to prevent having to weed, and to get the area covered within a year instead of having to wait for five. If the patch ends up looking too crowded after a while, simply remove some of the plants.

Pay attention to the plant's growth habit when planting your rose. A variety like 'Bassino' grows flat; it reaches only about 30 cm (12") high and will be at most 40 cm (14") wide, so while it's an ideal rose for edging a flowerbed, it's the worst option for covering the ground of a large slope. It should be planted in groups of at least five per square meter (11 sq ft). 'Fru Dagmar Hastrup' is a very popular and hardy species rose often used as groundcover that can reach a good meter (3') in height and 50 cm (20") wide. It's typically planted in groups of three per square meter (11 sq ft); as with the popular 'The Fairy' it should not be crowded with more than four plants per square meter (11 sq ft). My very own favorite, 'Flower Carpet', grows to at least 80 cm (32") wide and reaches 80 cm (32") tops, depending on its location.

'Fru Dagmar Hastrup' is a hardy and handsome groundcover.

'Fairy Dance' at the front of a somewhat messy rose bed. New roses that are planted each year must prove their mettle and show survival skills by blooming without protest and not attracting disease before they can be relocated to a permanent spot in the garden.

Roses as groundcover for the flowerbed

Groundcover roses make great companion flowers—they are attractive edging and underplantings to other, taller flowers in a flowerbed. Low to the ground, they bloom abundantly and thrive among the taller bedding roses; they provide many more opportunities to combine beautiful colors and interesting varieties. The possibilities are endless—just give it a go. When planting many roses together, it's best to do so in formation—the lower groundcovers are set in a zigzag pattern in front of the upright roses—as this fills the space in more fully, the roses will have more room to spread (even though the spacing is the same), and it ends up looking more attractive.

Taking care of groundcover roses

Groundcover roses are very easy to care for. Really, there's hardly anything to it. The plants are low and close together, so they will hopefully strangle most of the weeds. In early spring, simply cut away damaged or dead branches, and fertilize and irrigate the healthy ones to encourage proper growth. Groundcover roses are not as vulnerable to cold as upright bedding roses, so in areas with snow you should be able to incorporate more varieties than only the roses proven hardy for that particular growing zone. Even if they're only considered hardy to zone 3 to 4, they will survive in colder zones if they're protected from the wind by a proper layer of snow. You can also cover the plants; in the fall, mound soil around the plant and place a few layers of fir branches on top, and the plant will be fine. It's not a good idea to let the rose canes freeze each year, because that negates the rose's purpose as groundcover. The canes should survive and spread out from year to year so the ground stays covered and weeds are kept at bay. If the ground is bare in the spring because the canes are frostbitten, then weeds will take the opportunity to sprout before new rose canes have a chance cover the ground again. To be on the safe side, if you're not sure the rose variety you've selected is hardy to the winter in your area, cover the branches if there's no snow cover. It will protect the rose and will save you the hassle of having to prune off dead canes.

Pruning low-growing and groundcover roses

Low-growing roses, whether groundcovers or sprawling in growth habit, need very little trimming. They're meant to grow larger and larger, and to keep spreading out. Many roses grow long, snaking canes that sprout upright at first; once long enough, they drop down again. The only pruning needed is done on dead or damaged canes. Canes growing the wrong way, canes that have been stepped on, or canes growing out onto the pathway, patio, or deck can be shortened, but should not be cut off entirely. Groundcover roses with long canes on the ground can take root so don't remove these either, just trim them.

These types of roses are commonly used in public gardens and spaces. They're cut down almost completely at regular intervals every few years to help refresh the roses. You can do this in your home garden, too; keep in mind however that this opens the door for weeds to grow between the plants, so you'll need to weed diligently.

The glossy green foliage of 'Sommermärchen' shows that it is disease resistant.

The stuff of dreams: masses of climbing roses, together with bedding roses and other flowers. This kind of flowerbed requires lots of water and nutrients in order to flower so luxuriously, as it gets both dry and hot close to a house's outer wall.

CLIMBING ROSES

Climbers are roses that have especially long canes, but in every other respect are similar to bedding roses. They come in a variety of shapes, sizes, and colors, so pick a rose according to how you intend to incorporate it into your garden. These roses don't actually climb; the canes' thorns (also referred to as prickles) hook onto one another and work their way upward. The prickles serve as a kind of climbing support, but not very good ones. Climbing roses do need additional help to grow skyward and flower abundantly.

Climbing roses are stunning to behold. Vigorous growers typically bloom only once; they can be used on arbors, pergolas, porches, and fences. Most climbers are pretty hardy, and are the type of rose best suited to the climate in the north of Sweden.

Lower climbers often have more elegant flowers and are 'remontant,' i.e. they flower several times or continuously over summer. Certain mid-climbers are also used as large shrubs, or can be tied to a trellis.

How fully they grow and develop will depend on both variety and climate. In the south of Sweden, a rose might grow as rapidly as a weed, overtaking the entire wall of a house, while in the north you'd be thankful if that same flower covered the surface of a small trellis. The length of summer is also a contributing factor. In the south of Sweden roses start growing in April; in a colder climate they don't begin in earnest until the month of July.

Choosing the right rose

Climbers are a mixed bag, since they're the end result of the hybridization of many, many varieties. They can either flower on the current year's new shoots, or on small shoots from the previous year's canes. This will have some bearing on the rose's hardiness, blooming period, and abundance, and will determine whether they'll flower continuously over the summer. 'Ramblers' are roses with long flexible

Wonderful yet short-lived here, 'Valdemar' blooms only once, but how dreamy it is when it does.

'Awakening', a full rose from the incredibly popular and hardy 'New Dawn'.

Climbers with traits of species roses—for pergolas and arbors

Honungsros (honey rose), from the *Rosa helenae* group, are vigorous and popular roses; all flower once. The Swedish name describes the sweet scent of honey emitted by the yellowy white flowers. It blooms intensely for one week at the onset of summer. These roses grow extremely vigorously in the southern parts of Sweden. They're excellent for arbors and porches; they became very popular at the beginning of the 1990s.

'Aksel Olsen' is a single flower variety that sets clusters of many small hips.

'Hybrida' features double to semi-full whitish yellow flowers. The buds are slightly yellow, but the opened flower fades very quickly to white. It sets plenty of hips and is considered somewhat hardier than other varieties.

The Danish rose 'Lykkefund' also has semi-full flowers collected in large clusters, but it sets far fewer hips than others. It's hardy in Swedish zone 3, 'Hybrida' in zones 4–5.

'Polstjärnan', *Rosa beggeriana*, is our most hardy climbing rose, and is found throughout northern Sweden and Finland. It flowers once and then sets rosehips; hardy in Swedish zones 6–7.

'Venusta Pendula' of the *Rosa arvensis* group is most likely a very old climbing rose. This strong specimen was re-introduced by the German company Kordes in 1928. It blooms only once with full white flowers with a pink luster. It lacks scent and is very susceptible to powdery mildew. It's hardy in Swedish zones 3–4.

canes that grow from the base of the plant, and flower on the current year's shoots. They're often non-repeaters (non-remontant) with many small flowers. Roses with permanent stiff branches upon which grow yearly short flower shoots are called 'Climbers'. They usually flower repeatedly—or even continuously, as in the case of 'Sympathie'. This classification can become a bit blurry, however, because certain varieties can be considered ramblers as well as climbers. One such rose is 'New Dawn' which, after its main bloom, throws in sprinklings of flowers in late summer.

Separating climbing roses into several groups can be quite a complex undertaking, as there are species roses, historical roses, and modern beauties. It's impossible to generalize by saying that older varieties or species roses are hardier than newer ones, because that will vary from type to type. Grouping roses is not really that relevant, with the exception of some exhibiting more specific traits. The most important information to keep in mind is the rose's growth habit and the height it will ultimately reach.

Historical climbers

Rosa multiflora and *Rosa wichurana* are two groups of climbers. *Rosa multiflora* is a species rose climbing shrub. It grows long flexible canes, and blooms once with small white flowers. This rose is still commonly encountered as it's used as rootstock (also called under stock) for climber roses and bedding roses. *Rosa multiflora* suckers can often be seen growing among climbing roses. See 'Problem roses', p. 148.

Rosa wichurana varieties differ markedly from one another; some bloom with large flowers and others with small flowers. Most of them are non-repeaters, but 'New Dawn' returns with a sprinkling of flowers at the end of the season. They flower on the previous year's canes, and therefore require very careful pruning. If the canes freeze, there will be no flowers the following season, so it's best to cover them up during winter in colder climates. According to rose growers, 'New Dawn' is a best seller worldwide; it's much admired in Sweden, especially further north. 'New Dawn', the sport of another climber, has now become the parent to many large-flowered climbing roses such as 'Penny Lane'. The newly introduced 'Awakening' is, in turn, a full rose, sport of 'New Dawn'.

Big, vigorously growing roses that are suited to arbors, porches and pergolas are close relatives of the species rose. They're typically non-repeaters that produce a huge amount of small flowers. Climbing roses

Honungsros, 'Rosa Helenae Hybrida', is extraordinarily flower-rich and vigorous, with an amazing one-time bloom in early summer. Unfortunately, it's not a very hardy plant; some varieties make it in central Sweden, but this extravagant flower show can most often be seen in the south of Sweden.

with species rose traits are typically sold under their botanical name, not just the variety's name on the label. However, don't let complicated or scientific names scare you off as it's quite easy to find the right variety once you're in the garden center or nursery.

Old-fashioned beauty

You can still find some of the older climbing roses for sale, but they aren't many left anymore. Noisette roses grow like climbers or shrubs and are non-repeaters. They once held people rapt, as there were fewer climbers then than there are today, especially yellow ones. They're not very hardy—only in Swedish zones 1–2. A few exceptionally beautiful heirloom varieties have survived the push towards modern hybrids and are still available on the market, even though they exhibit many flaws compared to contemporary climbing roses.

'Gloire de Dijon', from 1879, is one such climber that has remained very popular. The flowers are large, full and nearly spherical, but open up to become flat. They have a wonderful apricot color, and are so heavy that they nod as soon as they flower on last year's shoot.

'Mme Alfred Carrier' is another survivor, a vigorous grower also dating back to 1879. The early summer rich bloom consists of small, very light pink—almost white—flowers. It repeats later in the season but in lesser quantities. The flowers sit on thin stems and nod. Suits Swedish zones 2–3.

This lively 'Gloire de Dijon' was planted on the Swedish island of Hven in 1919. It's listed under the heading Tea Roses in the catalogue from L. Larssons Rosen & Trädskolor (Sweden) dated 1911. There are six varieties listed under ramblers, none of which are known to us today.

Modern climbing roses

Elegant, modern climbing roses started appearing in the 1950s. They are related to old-fashioned varieties but produce large magnificent flowers in a wide range of colors. They are beauties in their own right but aren't robust in their growth habit, making them suitable to grow on trellises, garden obelisks and smaller arches. Modern roses, with their attractive large blooms, are called large-flowered climbing roses, but there are also many new varieties with simpler flowers, too. Some new rose specimens are somewhere between climbers and shrubs. In colder climates they tend to be more shrub-like, while in milder environments where the growing period is longer, they often turn into climbers.

Assortment of climbing roses

The range of climbing roses is large compared to what was available twenty years ago, but still not nearly as expansive as for bedding and shrub roses. Garden centers often sell white, yellow, pink, and apricot-orange roses alongside the occasional climbing rose like *Rosa helenae* 'Hybrida', which exhibits more of a species profile. If you're interested in finding a bigger selection or discovering new varieties, you'll have to do some research first and then place an order with a specialty retailer that offers a wide range of product. Best selling varieties of roses and the more common specimens in our gardens generally date back to the 1950s. You may find a few newer types; however, many recent arrivals have not yet become popular in Sweden. There's a distinct shortage of warm pink and of orange climbers; a truly hardy white variety with continuous blooms does not exist yet.

Extra hardy climbing roses

Foreign catalogues or books about climbing roses feature a lot of newer varieties, but many of them don't seem to be able to make it in our climate. It's not as easy to cultivate a climbing rose in a cold climate as it is in a milder one. One advantage of a colder climate, however, is that roses tend to stay healthier and in good shape. Flowering is short but intense, and the long daylight hours produce very intense colors. Sadly, few varieties tolerate the winter weather.

Aside from hardy, non-repeating climbing roses, there's another group of sturdy varieties that repeat-bloom several times. They're the product of hybridization with the *Rosa rugosa* rambler 'Max Graf', and are known under the name Kordesii roses. They're medium large climbers and high shrubs, and are considered disease resistant, hardy and robust. Some of them are, in fact, the best repeat-bloom climbing roses currently available to anyone gardening in a colder zone.

'New Dawn' is one of the hardiest climbing roses available. It's popular throughout Sweden with its profusion of blooms in early summer and sprinklings of flowers in the fall, as the weather allows.

'Hansaland' is a newer climbing rose that seems to be hardy, resilient, and a robust grower. This variety is well worth a try. Here, it grows harmoniously with a Rosa rugosa hedge.

Common climbing roses for cold climates

'Etude' produces glossy leaves, large, half-full deep pink flowers with a hint of scent. It flowers nearly continuously through the summer. Can also be grown as a bush. Swedish zone 5.

'Flammentanz' is the best red climber for cold climates. Flowers on last year's shoots; Swedish zone 6.

'Hybrida' is the hardiest *Rosa helenae*. Suitable for planting alongside trees, porches and to cover arches. A non-repeater for Swedish zone 5 (see picture, p. 57)

'Hansaland' is an interesting climber with attractive *Rosa rugosa*-type red coloring. Not too tall, around 2 meters (6½'); it's very hardy; probably Swedish zone 5 or colder.

'Hurdalsrosen' (Alba hybrid) is medium pink; hardy in Swedish zone 7.

'Leverkusen' is the hardiest of the yellow roses. Its color fades quickly but attractively. Swedish zone 5.

'Jolly Danse' (also known as 'Emilie') is an apricot-colored sport of 'Leverkusen', and is just as hardy. It's difficult to find, but it is being cultivated.

'New Dawn' has light pink, almost white flowers. Grows large and sturdy with glossy foliage. It blooms on new year's growth. Swedish zone 5.

'Polstjärnan' (*Rosa* 'Polstjärnan' Rosaceae) is the hardiest of the climbing roses. It is a non-repeater with many small white flowers. Swedish zone 7.

So far, 'Flammentanz' is the most successful climbing rose in the north of Sweden.

At right: 'Alchemyst' is an older variety that is, unfortunately, a non-repeater.

Red climbing roses are extremely popular, and 'Sympathie' is the best seller of the repeaters.

'Penny Lane' is propagated from 'New Dawn' rose seed, and has retained the same lovely color.

The most common climber varieties at garden centers and nurseries

Name	Color	Swedish zone
'Aloha'	Shrub/climber; non-repeater, yellow-apricot-pink full flower	3
'Boogie-Woogie'	Shrub/climber; generous first bloom of intense pink flowers, followed by a sprinkling later on	3
'Coral Dawn'	Salmon pink version of 'New Dawn'; not as hardy	2–3
'Dortmund'	Single red with white eye	3–4?
'Golden Showers'	Yellow	4
'Goldener Olymp'	Dark yellow	3
'Grand Hotel'	Red	3
'Händel'	Bicolor white and pink	2–3
'Ilse Krohn Superior'	White	3
'Penny Lane'	Light pink elegant flower	3
'Rosarium Uetersen'	Pink with a hint of salmon	3
'Santana'	Red	2–3
'Schneewaltzer'	White	2–3
'Sympathie'	Red	3–4

'Dortmund' is a Kordesii rose that will repeat-bloom several times if deadheaded.

The Canadian rose 'Henry Kelsey' is used both as a shrub and a climber.

'Flammentanz' is a very common rose that often puts on a magnificent and drawn-out flower show.

Above, 'Laguna' and below, 'Jasmina', are two new varieties in the series Climbing Max.

Canadian climbing roses

In Canada, the hardy Kordesii roses have been used to produce new, hardier specimens. At this point it is difficult to predict how well these newer roses are going to fare, but several of them can be used as both shrubs and climbers.

Canadian climbing roses

Name	Red roses	Swedish zone
'John Cabot'	double, pinkish red climbing shrub; 2–3 m (2½'–4')	5
'Henry Kelsey'	pinkish red, semi-double with long bloom time, climber/shrub	5
'William Baffin'	strong repeater in pinkish red, robust growth habit, 2–3 m (2½' - 4')	5–6
'William Booth'	double red flower; repeater; 2–3 m (2½'–4')	5

Newer climbing roses

The beginning of the twenty-first century has seen several interesting German and Danish varieties emerge in quick succession. Climbing Max is a completely new group of climbers from the German company Kordes, and several of its varieties have a more old-fashioned flower shape. Although still untested in Sweden, they look promising since most hardy climbing roses come from specimens used to produce these new flowers. They're well worth trying in Swedish zones 3–4.

Newer climbing roses

Name	Color	Height
'Amadeus'	This luminously red flower is not totally new, but is unknown in Sweden. Very faint fragrance.	2 m (6½')
'Amaretto'	Lovely pink with a hint of apricot. In Germany it reaches 2½ m (+8').	2½ m (+8')
'Jasmina'	Charming deep pink and round, very full nodding flowers, reaches 2 m (6½') even when grown as a shrub.	2 m (6½')
'Laguna'	Full, old-fashioned cupped flower in deep pink. Sweet scent and very disease resistant.	2½ m (+8')
'Rosanna' (6½')	An older type with salmon-pink, high-centered flowers. Highly disease resistant but lacks fragrance.	2 m
Kordes 'Rose Aloha' (+8')	A new variety with an old name. This 'Rose Aloha' has a warm yellow-pink-orange shade with a hint of fragrance.	2½ m

'White Nights' is a climber with high-centered flowers. This type of white climber is very much in demand, but there aren't many varieties to choose from that work well in Sweden.

'Rosenholm' is a relatively new climbing rose that can grow up to 3 to 4 meters (10' to +14') high in the south of Sweden. Hardiness is still unproven, but such lavish blooms rightly deserve a place in the garden. Perfect for a pergola, a porch and larger trellises.

A diminutive garden in Landskrona, Sweden, produces an abundance of flowers. Climbing roses don't take up a lot of ground space. The planting hole only needs to be 50 cm (slightly more than 1½') in diameter and depth, and the roots will spread under the stone-paved ground and the fencing. Balcony flower boxes filled with geraniums and cascading water hyssop make a delightful match with the roses.

Medium-sized climbing roses

Courtyard roses are a newer group of climbing roses. They can all be used as either climbers or shrubs, with support. One of them, 'Rosenholm', is said to reach a height of 2 to 3 m (6½' to +10') but in Denmark it definitely grows taller, and is exceptionally lovely. Its flower is reminiscent of 'The Fairy'; see picture, p. 65. All varieties in this group emit a faint scent and are repeat bloomers during the summer. The novelty here is in their flower habit. Climbing roses are typically pretty sparse on flowers in their lower section, but Courtyard roses set flowers all the way from the bottom up. Their hardiness is uncertain. Below is a selection of specimens in this group; new varieties are introduced every year and work is ongoing to produce flowers in apricot orange and white, both of which are eagerly anticipated.

Medium-sized climbers

Name	Color	Height
'Bolero'	single, white with some pink	2–3 m (6½' to +10')
'Boogie-Woogie'	half-full, light reddish pink	1½–2 m (5' to 6½')
'Flashdance'	small, full, dark yellow	1½–2 m (5' to 6½')
'Night Light'	large, yellow-red-orange flowers	1½–2 m (5' to 6½')
'Northern Lights'	double, light pink	1½–2 m (5' to 6½')
'Rosenholm'	small, half-full, baby pink	2–3 m (6½' to +10')
'Rhythm N Blues'	half-full, pink	2–2½ m (6½' to + 8')
'That's Jazz'	large, full, red	2–2½ m (6½' to + 8')
'Twist'	half-full, pink and white stripes	1½–2 m (5' to 6½')
'White Nights'	large, full, white high-centered flowers	2–2½ m (6½' to + 8')
'Zorba'	small, full, yellowish pink	1½–2 m (5' to 6½')

Caring for climbing roses

While caring for climbing roses isn't trickier than for any other type of climbing plant, what is special about climbing roses is that a lot of debris collects in the canes. If the rose is grown against a wall, old leaves, dust, pollen and petals, as well as insect ova, don't get blown off easily, so all kinds of pests and eggs thrive in the wall's warmth and protection. Even fungal diseases, which normally freeze off during the winter, can overwinter in a good spot, so clean your roses thoroughly in fall by sweeping up the debris and snip off any damaged parts. Do not leave old flowers and withered leaves on the plant.

Pruning climbing roses

Climbing roses that grow against a wall turn green earlier than bedding roses. They need to be pruned slightly earlier in the season than the bedding roses, but how much earlier depends on location and local climate. If they've spent winter covered in fir branches, it'll be time to prune them as soon as they start growing leaves behind those branches.

Climbing roses should be thinned out and pruned a little each year to encourage fuller blooming. Remove one (or several, as the case may be) of the oldest canes off the plant—they're thicker, greyer or browner, with peeling bark, and they often lack thorns. Cut them off at 10 to 20 cm (4" to 8") from the ground. If it stays unpruned, the rose will still eventually flower, but produce fewer blooms.

Climbing roses should be pruned a little each year. A few older canes are removed to leave room for new and eager shoots to grow.

'Aloha' accompanied by hollyhocks. They will provide color when the first flush of the rose bloom has faded.

Hardy yellow climbing roses are scarce. 'Leverkusen' is one of the sturdier specimens that are currently available, but it fades fairly quickly. Make sure to try some of the newcomers that will be on the market in the near future.

One way to incorporate companion plants into your rose garden is with a container of summer flowers, as with the lilies shown here. The pot protects the soil around the rose's roots, and when it has finished blooming, the lilies step in to provide attractive color.

Training climbing roses

The time to train a climbing rose is early in springtime, before the plant turns green. Top prune the long shoot so that the rose grows evenly over the space you want it to cover. Deadhead young shoots that look like long, prickly twigs, and that are visibly green, brown, or red with smooth bark. Remove canes that grow in the wrong direction, that protrude, or that are otherwise in the way. A rose will typically grow towards the sun, so even out the plant by training canes to grow in the opposite direction.

A climber needs to be fastened pretty flat up against its support in order to promote abundant flowering. The canes are tied onto their support inch by inch over the summer, while they're still soft and pliable. They'll also need to be securely bound during winter while their shape is still discernible. If not trained, the canes continue to grow around themselves and end up forming a larger and wider mass that could eventually make the plant keel over or buckle under its own size and weight. Also, a large overhanging plant overshadows its lower canes, preventing new young flowers from producing shoots on that part of the plant.

Irrigation and fertilizing

Climbing roses are large and vigorous plants that require more water and nutrients than bedding roses. Use a watering can to give each plant 20 to 30 liters (5 to 8 gallons) of water at least once a week. Make sure there's an edge along the flowerbed to catch the water to make for easier irrigation. Large plants usually have deep roots, so they will manage well without water for a spell—if there isn't an extreme drought, that is. Young, newly planted roses, however, need regular irrigation at the onset, for two to three years.

Climbing roses might need extra fertilizing; 1 ml (0.03 fl oz) of the Swedish fertilizer Blomstra (or local equivalent) per quart of water should encourage a good growth spurt. Stop fertilizing once fall sets in—late July or August, depending on your location—when the rose needs to stop growing.

Climbing roses in cold climates

Not all climbing roses need to be covered in winter; nonetheless it's good practice to protect them in cold climates and if the roses are blooming on growth from the previous year. Thread a large quantity of small fir branches through the canes over the entire plant; this shields it from the elements better than you'd expect, and many small pieces are more likely to stay in place than a few big ones.

You can also protect the plant with a burlap cover, or hang a shadow cloth in front of the whole climbing rose. Wrap an untrained rose in burlap and pile soil up around its base like you would for bedding roses, and shove some fir branches into the earth in front of the plant. Another way would be to blanket the plant with leaves, then place fir branches on top to keep them all in place.

Once spring rolls around, keep a cool head and refrain from uncovering your roses too early, because the combination of warm sunny days and frosty nights is deadly to climbers. Shoots emerge from the canes behind the protective covering, which is when they really need to be protected from low nighttime temperatures. Only remove the cover or the fir branches and prune the rose when you're certain beyond a doubt that spring has finally sprung. Start watering early if the rose grows under a protruding roof, since the soil is likely to drain quickly and dry up much faster along the side of a house.

Companion plants to climbing roses

Climbing roses reach upward to become tall plants, and are quite sparse in flowers near the ground. Filling in the empty areas on the ground with other plants near the base of the rose prevents the sun from drying out the soil and hardening its surface; this also keeps the soil loose and makes it more receptive to water. Low-growing roses, perennials, annuals, shrubs, and other climbers all make excellent companion plants; simply pick plants that thrive in the same environment as the roses.

Clematis varieties

Climbing roses are beautiful by themselves, but other plants can definitely bring something to the party.

Not only is it possible to group other plants with climbing roses, but it is actually recommended. Here, a rose is planted next to an everlasting sweet pea (a perennial without fragrance), and luminously blue delphiniums.

Roses and clematis are a classic combination that can be as varied as there are colors. Here, with clematis 'Hagley Hybrid'.

Finn Eldh, an expert on clematis, likes to see roses as companions to clematis. Not merely a complement to non-repeating roses, they can also add great color to the show when blooming in tandem with roses. One of his finest combinations is blue clematis 'Luther Burbank' with red 'Sympathie', which bloom simultaneously in July.

Varieties of clematis

A special characteristic of clematis is that different varieties flower at different times. There are spring-flowering types with nodding bells; late blooming varieties in the fall; and elegant, large-flowered summer blossoms in between. Late-summer bloomers typically flower on new branches that grow during the summer, so they're ideal to grow with climbing roses. The following varieties come recommended by Finn Eldh of the Swedish Clematis Society. They're pruned in late fall and have large, flat flowers.

'Black Prince', a simple, almost black-red flower. Hails from New Zealand.

'Blue Angel' (**'BlekitnyAniol'**), a sky-blue beauty with crepe-paper like flowers; from Poland.

'Emilia Plater', has slightly bluer shade.

'Esperanto', has a very large, graceful, dark pinkish red flower.

'Kotkas', white, star like flowers, more than 25 cm (nearly 10") in diameter, with outward middle pink stripes.

'Luther Burbank', far superior to 'Jackmanii', even though it is similar in looks with dark lilac flowers.

'Pulmapäev', is white and the most beautiful of them all. The name means **'Wedding Day'**.

'Pöhjanel' is the breeder's own favorite; a blue flower with reddish lilac middle stripe. Reminiscent of the less hardy 'Dr. Ruppel'.

'Ristimägi', blue flowers with slight reddish lilac star in the center.

'Triinu', a lighter pinkish red flower with dark middle stripe.

'Valge Daam', a white, nearly bluish white favorite with a white center, for very special effect. The name means 'the white lady'.

'Viola', is one of the best deep blue varieties, and is a very profuse bloomer.

Since many of the flowering climbing roses are not reliably hardy in central and northern Sweden, their best companions in those areas are the non-repeaters. For example, combine a climbing rose with late-summer flowering clematis to add an extra pop of color. A wide selection of wonderful clematis is available on the marketplace, sometimes making it difficult to decide which clematis to buy, as well as making it challenging to identify accurately. Typically, the clematis container comes with a plastic label that includes a color picture, the flip side telling you what species of clematis it is. 'Jackmanii' and *viticella* varieties bloom on this year's shoots; they belong to pruning group 3, summer flowering in July to September, and are most suited to be planted with roses. Estonian and Polish varieties are becoming more common in Sweden; by all means, go ahead and try them if they're available in your area. Many belong to group 3; they're easily identifiable by their names; both are hardy, disease resistant and a delight to behold.

Another option is to plant a clematis particularly well adapted to Sweden, like the following late-summer flowering varieties: 'Carmencita' with flat wine-red flowers, 'Södertälje' with pendulous dark red open bells, and 'Mrs T. Lundell' with a violet-blue, four-petal open flower. They are all quite hardy and easy to care for in up to Swedish zone 4.

Planting roses and clematis

Clematis, like roses, need plenty of water and nutrients. Do not plant them together in the same planting hole—you need to separate them a little. Neither of them will thrive by a wall in southern exposure, with their roots in the drainage under a jutting roof. Plant them approximately 50 cm (1½') from the house's exterior, then guide the branches from the plant towards the trellis on the wall. The trellis needs to be installed with brackets to keep it 15 to 20 cm (6" to 8") away from the wall, which allows air to circulate between the wall and the trellis. Both the planting holes for the clematis and the rose need to be dug deep until the grafting bud sits 7 to 10 cm (2¾" to 4") below the surface of the ground. Also, the harder the ground, the bigger and deeper the hole needs to be, as this will provide both rose and clematis with more porous soil to grow in. If you dig a big hole and set both plants in it together, you'll need to add a root barrier between the plants; see more on the subject in 'Planting alongside trees,' p. 72.

You need to pay attention to the vigor and growth habit of a climbing rose's companion plant. Honeysuckle and a climbing rose is a great combination, but only if the rose is a robust climber and the honeysuckle less so. Silver lace vine and Montana clematis are both too vigorous and threaten to smother the climbing rose entirely, putting an end to its growth and flowering.

Planting climbing roses next to old trees will coax more flowers from the garden. The rose enjoys structural support, while the tree gets new greenery.

Pruning clematis

One notable problem with using clematis as companion plants is pruning. A climbing rose needs to be thinned out only a little, and typically doesn't get any big cuts. Clematis, however, which flowers in late summer and fall, benefits most from being pruned every year. Trim it down to 20 to 30 cm (8" to 12") above the ground in late fall; go ahead and pile the soil up around the trunks of the rose and the clematis while you're at it. Hold off until spring to clean away the branches of the clematis; all the debris can be removed from it when the rose is being pruned so the two plants can start growing again. After this clean up, new nice shoots will grow from the bottom of the clematis and climb its way up the rose.

Other beautiful companion plants

There are many other climbers and companion plants for climbing roses, provided they share a similar growth habit to the rose. Things can become problematic with aggressive climbers such as the Montana clematis or silver lace vine (in Sweden also called 'The architect's solace'), as they often end up strangling the rose. The best way to find good companions is to 'audition' different plants and make sure they all get what they need in terms of water and nutrients. By making deep planting holes and by using root barriers you can ensure that both plants get their fair share of resources, at least during the first year. Even annuals can make good companion plants for climbing roses;

simply place them in a pot in front of the rose and they'll get plenty of what they need without having to compete with the rose.

The natural charm of informal growth

Climbing roses can also be used in a more naturalistic, informal way in the garden. Roses that climb up into trees or other large plants add a charming and luxuriant look to the landscape. However, roses that are robust enough to climb up into other plants might also do them harm, so you have to use caution when selecting companion plants. It would be sad to see a beautiful blooming lilac taken down by a tough rose; by the same token, a weaker rose would not have the strength to climb up the lilac and would be done in by its competition. Climbing roses tend to do well next to trees, especially older ones that are in decline, because they provide necessary support that reaches far into the sky; they're also freestanding, which means that the climber is exposed to sunshine from all sides, which allows it to grow and thrive.

Planting alongside trees

You'll need to make sure that your roses can cope when you plant them alongside trees. An existing bush or tree has already set down plenty of roots in the ground, so your rose will require some assistance to make its own roots develop and spread out without too much interference. A twenty-five to thirty-year old tree with a deep and established root system will have a clear advantage over the rose's small and delicate roots, so inserting a root barrier will prevent the established plant's roots from siphoning all water and nutrients away from the new rose. The rose's planting hole should be dug at least 50 to 100 cm (1½' to 3') away from the neighbor plant, and it must be larger than the rose's roots—approximately 50 to 70 cm (1½' to 2¼') deep. The root barrier, a dense cloth that roots can't penetrate, is set down on the side of the other plant's roots, and should reach all the way to the bottom of the planting hole (you can also use a vinyl cloth or a plastic sheet as root barrier). Plant the rose in the usual way, and lead it to the support plant with strings or stakes. It might be necessary at first to tie the rose canes to the larger plant so it doesn't blow down or break. Irrigate and fertilize on the rose's side of the root barrier. Water carefully, because the rose will need all the help it can get at the beginning; later on it will do just fine. The same applies to planting clematis next to an already established rose, in which case the rose is the stronger plant and the clematis is the newcomer needing a helping hand.

A climbing rose that has grown in the same spot for many years has a strong set of roots going deep down in the ground. When planting a new rose, you should water it every week to give the rose an auspicious beginning.

'Parkzierde', an old-fashioned shrub rose, is surrounded here by foxglove and oxeye daisies—also called marguerites—that spread at will. The shrubs are so robust that they're not bothered that their companion plants are making themselves comfortable.

ROSES AS SHRUBS

Park roses and shrub roses are plants grown as ornamental shrubs. They can flower several times, and more or less continuously. These are wonderful roses that are even easier to care for than bedding roses, but they don't have quite the same visual impact.

Many of the old-fashioned roses that are so popular are, in fact, shrub roses. In spite of the image that the name brings to mind, shrub roses can be both large and small. Many shrubs grow very large while others don't get any bigger than a sturdy bedding rose. Many species roses, like Eglantine rose and *Rosa canina*, are also shrub roses. Many of them are resilient and hardy, and can easily be both ornamental and provide protection.

A distinction is made between bedding roses and roses that are used as ornamentals. It's not a strict partition, however; it's based more on location, taste and personal preferences. Shrub roses are larger and sturdier elements in the garden, whereas bedding roses are more like perennials; it's a good idea to know what type of rose you're dealing with before choosing a shrub. Knowing their correct botanical name is important, and naming is not as tricky as it is with other roses. Varieties within the same group typically share common characteristics.

Shrub roses are usually more wild-looking, and are eminently suitable to a more naturalistic landscape. In a mature setting, shrub roses might be more fitting, but here again it depends on the variety of roses. It wouldn't make sense to plant salmon orange or copper colored roses at an eighteenth-century cottage, because roses in those colors did not exist at the time when the cottage was built. On the other hand, old-world style modern roses with white flowers might work in such a garden, the difference being that modern roses bloom so much longer than roses did back in the 1700s. A really luminous red is another color to be cautious with in an older setting—older red roses always had a hint of purple in them, while modern roses are more starkly red.

'Frühlingsgold' is a modern variety of the burnet rose, and it flowers in early summer.

Wild and wonderful

Large shrub roses are close relatives of species roses. Among the hardiest types are the burnet, *Rosa rugosa*—also called Japanese Rose—and a few old roses like the antique Albas. They usually flower only once, but can bloom again with a sprinkling of flowers later on in the season. Many make lovely companion plants, but they can sometimes be a bit too large to include in a flowerbed.

The type of roses you choose depends on how they are to be planted; their ultimate size will depend on their location. A rose that will grow to 3 m (nearly 19') in the southern part of Sweden will most likely not reach higher than a modest single meter (3¼') in the north. If grown in a windy spot, *Rosa rugosa*—the Japanese rose—will only reach a height of about 75 cm (2½'), while if it's in a protected spot it can reach 2 m (6½'). The advantage of rose shrubs is that they can be used just like bushes. Most flowering ornamental bushes need a sunny location and nutrient rich soil. That's also a good setting for shrub roses, even if some of them can cope in less-than-perfect soil, in drought or windy conditions. Wet, heavy, compact, and clay-rich soils should be avoided.

Roses provide protection and support for other roses

It's nice to create companion plantings with shrub roses and other bushes to prolong the flowering period in the garden. Many of the traditional ornamental bushes, like lilacs and mock orange, flower in early summer, so shrub roses can add a much-needed spot of color once they have flowered out. In addition, many roses contribute attractive foliage and elegant rosehips to the garden. Shrub roses pair well with other roses, too—both bedding and groundcover varieties. A large shrub rose, once its flowers are spent, can be a green backdrop to lower-growing roses up front, and also provide them with some shelter if they're in a windy spot. Many shrub roses bloom early, before the bedding roses; large shrub roses also make excellent support for less sturdy climbers.

Resilient, old-fashioned ("grandmother") roses

The burnet rose—also known as the Scottish rose—is a popular traditional flower in older gardens; it was cultivated as early as the 1400s. This is a non-repeater with tough roses that can tolerate wind and less-than-perfect soil, and it blooms early. The burnet spreads easily and far by suckers, and is often full of stiff prickles. White and pink full flowers can be found in older gardens where they might have survived without care for over fifty to sixty years. They can be easily spotted with their distinct, bluish black rosehips and their small, fern-like leaves.

Pimpinellifolia 'Plena' (White Rose of Finland) has small, white full flowers and is very popular in the north of Sweden, where it is hardy to zone 7–8. Another popular and almost as hardy shrub rose is the 'Poppius' with its pink, semi-double marzipan-rose lookalike flowers.

Further improved varieties exist, like 'Aicha', a single yellow flower with a golden eye, which only blooms for a week but with flowers of brilliant beauty.

'Frühlingsduft', 'Frühlingsgold', and 'Frühlingsmorgen' are all German varieties with excellent, but short, bloom. They're large shrubs that make perfect companion plants to late-summer flowering clematis. The light pink 'Stanwell Perpetual' is popular, as it occasionally comes back with a sprinkling of flowers in the fall. All the above-mentioned are hardy to Swedish zone 5.

White and pink burnet (Scottish) roses can be found in many gardens. They're sometimes called Grandmother roses, and they spread by suckers from garden to garden. These roses are survivors—resilient and hardy.

'Ritausma' is a charmer of a Rosa rugosa, *with full somewhat nodding flowers. Lamb's ear and catchfly are in the companion planting.*

A rose hip hedge of coastal roses

Rosa rugosa, also called Japanese rose, has its origins in China and Japan. Rugosa roses are easily recognizable with their shiny green, somewhat wrinkly leaves. Their main characteristics are their health, hardiness and their multitudes of large prickles. Rugosas bloom early and typically set large flat round orange hips. They repeat bloom all summer, and also have some sprinkles of flowers in the fall; many varieties flower and bear hips simultaneously. Rugosas can be found in the family trees of many modern roses, as it was introduced to make the modern roses hardier and more disease resistant. Most rugosa varieties are pinkish mauve or white in color, and flowers come in forms from single to full. They are hardy in Swedish zone 4 and up to 7 or 8, depending on variety. Many rugosas will endure salt, wind, drought, and poor growing locations. They're excellent used as hedges, bushes, groundcovers, for wind protection, and to control the erosion of sandy soil.

Rugosa roses have always been popular, but up until recently there haven't been many varieties to pick from on the market. Thanks to many new varieties that have come out of Canada in the late 1990s, there's now a wider selection to look at, and interest in these roses has increased markedly. To read more about Canadian roses, see p. 84–85.

'Agnes' has yellow, wonderful lemon scented flowers on an ugly shrub full of prickles that sets no hips. It was one of the first Canadian roses created at the Central Experimental Farm Ottawa in 1900. They began improving the *Rosa rugosas* in 1980, which are now being introduced. Hardy to Swedish zone 5.

'Blanc Double de Coubert' is beautiful, with pure white half-full flowers and shiny grass-green foliage. Swedish zone 6.

'Fru Dagmar Hastrup' is very common in public spaces. This low-growing large shrub with single, large open light pink flowers is used as groundcover. Swedish zone 6.

'Hansa' has double, mauve colored flowers. It grows into a robust and hardy shrub and can get quite tall; Swedish zone 6. See picture, p. 85.

'Hansaland', a rather new variety that can grow to 2 m (6½') in height, and can be used as a climber. It lacks scent but has an unusually red color for a *Rosa rugosa*.

'Moje Hammarberg', a Swedish rugosa variety with double blooms like 'Hansa' that doesn't grow quite as tall. Swedish zone 7.

'Ritausma' produces full, light pink nodding flowers. It is low-growing, a lovely edging rose, but only hardy to Swedish zone 4. See picture at the top of the page.

'Grootendorst' is a series of *Rosa rugosa* with completely different flowers; they look more like small carnations. 'F.J. Grootendorst' is reddish pink; see p. 78. The sport 'Pink Grootendorst' is baby pink and its sport 'White Grootendorst' is white. All are prolific bloomers and hardy to Swedish zone 5–6, maybe 7.

'Signe Relander', which has the same kind of flower but is a deeper red, is slightly less hardy than the other carnation roses.

Carnation rose is a Rosa rugosa *variety that was much in use in the 1960s. It's perfect in companion plantings and hedges since it's a prolific bloomer, very resiilient, and seldom attacked by disease.*

The foliage of Rosa glauca *embellishes a flowering lilac. Leaves and hips are decorative details to keep in mind when choosing roses.*

Elegant rose hips and beautiful foliage

Rosa moyesii grow tall, sprawling shrubs with lots of sharp prickles. They tolerate poor soil and cold climates. They develop large single flowers in early summer and then set very decorative hips. The bloom shades go from red to white while the original variety had bright reddish orange flowers.

'Geranium' is a beauty with a large, truly red flower, much reminiscent of a species rose. Very elegant rose hips. Hardy to Swedish zone 5.

'Nevada' is very popular in Sweden. It's a large shrub that produces large single flowers in pale yellow that fades to white. It occasionally brings back a sprinkling of flowers in the fall, but sets no hips. 'Margarete Hilling' is a pinkish 'Nevada' sport. Both are hardy to Swedish zone 5.

Rosa glauca (redleaf rose) is quite common. Very beautiful in hedges and shrubbery with its dewy greenish blue foliage. The 'Nova' E variety grows into a large shrub with semi-double flowers that flower slightly later than the roses that produce hips. This is a very resilient and hardy landscape rose; hardy to Swedish zone 6.

Yellow species roses

Rosa foetida from the group of the same name, was formerly incredibly popular as it was one of the few truly yellow roses. It flowers early, just once, on a sprawling bush with foliage similar to the burnet rose. Yellow is an uncommon color, and nearly all modern yellow and apricot colored flowers got their color from this rose. Unfortunately, another less desirable trait they've inherited from *Rose foetida* is a susceptibility to fungal disease.

'Bicolor', also called 'Capucine', is a species rose with single orange-red flower. Hardy to Swedish zone 5–6'.

'Persiana' has dark yellow double blooms. Its origin is unknown. Hardy to Swedish zones 5–6.

'Harison's Yellow' has semi-double to full yellow flowers. It's also known as yellow rose of Texas. It's still customary in Texas to have yellow roses in the bridal bouquet. 'Williams' Double Yellow' is very similar to 'Harison's Yellow'. Hardy to Swedish zone 5–6.

Rosa primula is the first of all roses to bloom. This is a large shrub that's covered in single flowers reminiscent of large buttercups. Absolutely enchanting in spring, beautiful as a shrub and in companion plantings. Somewhat arching canes and very wide. Hardy in Swedish zone 5.

Rosa hugonis is very similar to *Rosa primula* but blooms later. The canes, smothered in yellow single flowers, arch like a waterfall. It exists in double flower. Hardy to Swedish zone 5.

Living history

'Rose of Provins' or *Rosa gallica* is perhaps the first rose to be cultivated in Europe around 5,000 years ago. The Swedish name is provinsros ('Rose of Provins') but *Rosa gallica* is often used instead. *Rosa gallica* was cultivated for its petals, which were used for making rose water. The pinkish red or white flowers are strongly fragrant, and the rose flowers only once—at the turn of June to July. The rose's red color skews to mauve, and the flowers wither from red to grey violet. The shrub is often prone to developing mildew, and it produces plenty of suckers.

Rosa primula *blooms extremely early and produces an enchanting amount of flowers. The rose can be used in companion plantings and as a hedge, but it does grow very big.*

To have a Rosa officinalis *growing in the garden is a bit like owning a bit of living history. This rose has been cultivated as a medicinal plant for thousands of years.*

Rosa officinalis and *Rosa mundi*—the latter a stripy *Rosa officinalis*—were very common a long time ago. Both of these roses were probably growing in Tyco Brahe's (Danish astronomer, astrologer, alchemist, 1546–1601) garden in the 1590s, as they were considered to be medicinal plants and as such were cultivated in herb gardens. Both roses are hardy in Swedish zones 5–6 but will often freeze quite hard. There are many more Gallica names on the market, and they're all pretty similar flowers.

'Amiable Amie' has full baby-pink flowers and is hardy in Swedish zone 5.

'Belle de Crecy' has dark red-mauve flowers, often with a small eye. Swedish zone 5.

'Tuscany Superb', a dark wine red, improved version of 'Tuscany', which existed back in the 1500s.

The 'Damask' rose is believed to be a cross between *Rosa gallica* and *Rosa phoenicia*. The older varieties grow a rather large overhang of long thin canes; they were cultivated for the manufacture of rose oil, also called attar of rose. This is still done today, and many roses have a heady, beautiful scent.

'Rose de Rescht' is one of the best old-fashioned roses, and occasionally throws in a sprinkling of flowers once the rich summer bloom is over.

Rosa albas are healthy and hardy roses. In Sweden you can find full white varieties that have been grown in gardens for many years. Rosa alba is known in Sweden as a farm rose—it also has local, more colloquial names. Having been a part of our gardens for such a long time, they're the perfect candidate for an older red cottage garden setting, especially when you want to maintain the right character of the place.

'Leda' is easy to recognize and is very lovely. The flower itself is white but the bud and the back of the petals are stripy red. Hardy to Swedish zone 4.

'Mme Hardy', a beautiful white flower, considered by many as one of the finest white old-style roses. Swedish zone 5.

'Autumn Damask' ('Quatre Saisons') is the first rose to flower twice. They bloom heavily in early summer, and then repeat-bloom with a sprinkling if the first spent flowers are removed. 'Autumn Damasks' aren't especially hardy but 'Rose de Rescht', with its deep red flowers, is one of the best sellers among the old-world roses. It's hardy to Swedish zone 4.

A reliable small shrub

The Portland rose, from the *Rosa portlandica* group, is the offspring of the 'Autumn Damask' rose; it flowers twice. There are several good varieties with pink flowers that are suitable for a flowerbed. The shrubs grow rather low and round, and they're quite hardy. They work well as companion plants to modern roses, perennials and low bushes.

'Jacques Cartier' has pink flowers and is quite popular. Its flowers ebb and flow over a long period. 'Comte de Chambord', a pink rose, very famous among rose fanciers, is probably the same type as 'Mme Boll', yet both can be found on the market. All three are somewhat similar, and all emit scent. They're hardy to Swedish zone 4–5.

Big and Beautiful

Rosa albas are very hardy plants, but they too are non-repeaters. They grow beautifully, produce fine grey-green foliage, and can become quite large shrubs. They're very old roses, and they've been in Sweden a long time.

'Maxima' is probably the full white rose most often found in old Swedish gardens. It goes by colloquial names, one of which is farm rose. Hardiness is Swedish zone 5–7. There are several exquisite white alba roses; perhaps one of the Swedish names—jungfruros (virgin rose)—was meant to emphasize that the most beautiful roses are white.

'Mme Legras de St Germain' is known to be nearly free of prickles. It has a white full flower with a hint of yellow, especially when fully opened. It's hardy to Swedish zone 5.

'Mme Plantier' has a very full white flower with a hint of
pink, sometimes with an eye in the middle. The pink is
more visible in cooler weather. It's a lovely variety, and
hardy to Swedish zone 5.

'Maiden's Blush' is a very old variety with pale pink
flowers, and is hardy. It's believed to have been around
as early as the 1600s. Can tolerate some shade and is
hardy to Swedish zone 5.

Striking moss

Centifolia roses are known from Dutch paintings from the
1600s. Thousand-leaved rose, hundred-leaved/petaled
rose, Rose de Mai, Provence rose, and cabbage rose—all
are descriptive monikers of these roses. Their flowers are
very full and deeply cupped, but they only bloom once,
and don't repeat. The centifolia roses aren't very hardy,
and not even of much interest if it weren't for the moss
roses that emerge. Moss roses have a very specific look—
the scales that protect the buds are covered in green moss,
but even the canes can look mossy. These roses were
extremely popular during a period in the 1800s when
curiosities and 'freaks of nature' were all the rage. Most
moss roses are non-repeaters.

'Henri Matin' is a dark crimson red variety that's a very
worthwhile rose to set in difficult locations; and
tolerates some part-shade light. It's not a large shrub
but it's quite hardy; Swedish zone 4–5.

*The moss rose is perhaps considered more a curiosity rather
than beautiful, but there are many available on the market, and
'Henri Matin' is one of the best.*

*'Lichtkönigin Lucia' is a modern shrub rose, but it doesn't grow
into a true shrub. Like many other modern shrub roses, it's more
suited to the flowerbed.*

'Anna' is an unusual example because its breeding took place in Sweden. The goal is to produce healthy and hardy varieties.

'William Lobb' is a rather larger shrub. and even this is a resilient variety. Pinkish red, strongly scented flowers that wither into mauve. Swedish zone 4–5.

Elegant ladies

Some of the earliest hybridizing of European and Chinese roses gave us the Bourbon roses. The outcome is mixed, as most bourbon roses (but not all) are repeat blooming. Hardiness is also very uneven, and most specimens are sensitive to powdery mildew. The best varieties have scented, pinkish red blooms.

'Coupe de Hebe' has cupped full dark pink flowers that many consider to be the most beautiful roses of all.

'Louise Odier' is an incredibly popular rose with pink flowers and a lovely scent. Unfortunately, it's very susceptible to black spot. Nevertheless, it's a good choice for the northern part of Sweden where infections are less far-reaching. Hardy in Swedish zones 4–5.

'Souvenir de la Malmaison' produces muted pink flowers; sadly, the full flower buds have a tendency to rot in the rain.

'Ziegeunerknabe', or 'Gipsy Boy', was popular for a period of time, and can still be found in many older gardens; it's still around because it's so hardy. It flowers once with long-lasting deep mauve-red flowers. It's hardy in Swedish zone 5; see picture, p. 87.

'Wrams Gunnarstorp' is a pink climber that produces nodding flowers with high centers, and an abundant bloomer with repeating sprinkles of flowers in late summer. Its origin is unknown, but it was discovered at Vrams Gunnarstorp Castle where it had been growing for many years. Hardy in Swedish zones 2–3.

Train, climb or both

Musk rose, *Rosa moschata,* is a rose that can be found in many hybrids. Its fragrance is musk-like, and it blooms later and longer than many other roses. Musk roses grow tall and gangly, and can be trained like climbers or to hang over fences. They produce an overwhelming summer bloom containing many small flowers, and repeat with sprinkles of flowers. Varieties are often scented but they require quality soil and a good site; for many, hardiness is uncertain.

'Buff Beauty' is an incredibly beautiful rose with muted, apricot yellow large flowers; it's hardy in Swedish zone 2.

'Felicia' produces fluffy apricot/baby pink flowers; hardy in Swedish zone 3.

'Ghislaine de Feligonde' flowers abundantly in white over yellow to mild apricot. The buds have a strong orange/yellow tone, which heightens its beauty. This is one of the more popular climbing roses in the south of Sweden; in Swedish zone 3–4 it grows into a shrub.

'Mozart' is covered in small single cherry-pink flowers with a white eye. It's similar to 'Robin Hood', which has a deeper cherry-red color. Both are hardy to Swedish zone 4.

Scentless confusion

Rose breeding was extremely popular from 1850 up to the 1900s, a fad akin to the Dutch tulip mania of the 17th century. Many of the roses created during that period belong to a group called remontant roses. Remontant roses were given this name because they possess remontancy (from French 'remonter,' which means 'to come up again'), i.e. they flower more than once. Remontant roses have two specific flowering periods, while modern roses bloom continuously. More remontant roses emerged around the 1830s, and emphasis was given to each flower's appearance. There were rose breeding competitions, and people who showed roses were often the same people who

'Louis Bugnet' is a wonderful Rosa rugosa *that works in all areas of Sweden. It's healthy, hardy, a prolific bloomer, and is resilient to wind.*

competed in chrysanthemum and dahlia competitions. They were after the same kind of flowers—large, elegant and showy; fragrance was of no concern to them, and nobody cared about what the flower looked like once it wilted.

Hardiness and growth habit of plants also took a back seat to their looks. Since all these roses showed uneven hardiness at best and almost no disease resistance, there aren't many of these flowers still in existence out of all the thousands of varieties from that particular era.

One that has stood the test of time, however, is 'Empereur du Maroc'; its flowers are a very particular and stunning dark red color, but the shrub is ugly and often prone to disease. 'Ferdinand Richard' has extremely elegant reddish pink and white stripy flowers and lovely scent, but it too is susceptible to illness. 'Reine de Violettes' has a peculiar mauve color (the hunt for a true blue rose was on already by then) that withers into an intense greyish purple hue.

Today's shrub roses

Many large, scentless roses were launched in Sweden between the latter part of the 1800s and a good chunk of the 1900s, before the trend in rose breeding took a turn for the better. Today we can pick between old and new roses; scented or scentless flowers; single (non-repeater) and continuous flowering (repeaters); high or low-growing shrubs. If you're after shrubs that have large beautiful blooms that flower continuously through the summer, however, choice is still somewhat limited. There are far more options for those who live and garden in the southern part of Sweden than for those who live up north; for them, it's first and foremost the hardy *Rosa rugosa* that's available.

Modern shrub roses encompass roses that don't really fit into any other specific rose category. Canadian, Swedish, English, and many other roses belong to this group, so it's a very mixed bag with a misleading name. Don't get fooled into believing they're shrub roses solely because it says 'shrubs'; see picture on p. 81. When you buy roses to grow as shrubs, select varieties that are sufficiently sturdy and tall to really grow into shrubs.

'Adelaide Hoodless' is one of the hardy roses that belong to the group marketed as Canadian roses.

Canadian roses

Name	Description	Swedish zone
'Adelaide Hoodless'	P, rich red bloom in June, July, and August. Low shrub	5–6
'Alexander McKenzie'	Ex, deep red, flower, remontant, upright shrub	5–6
'Betty Bland'	Pink double flower, leaves have lovely fall color, height 1 to 2 m (3.25' to 6.5')	5
'Charles Albanel'	Ex, pinkish red full low-growing *Rosa rugosa*	5
'Cuthbert Grant'	P, upright red, remontant	5–6
'David Thompson'	Ex, *Rosa rugosa*, full mauve red, continuous bloom, height 1m (3.25')	6
'Henry Hudson'	Ex, *Rosa rugosa*, white, low and wide, height 50 cm (1.64')	6
'Henry Kelsey'	Ex, *Rosa rugosa*, pinkish/red flowers, climber/shrub rose	6
'Hope for Humanity'	P, new double, dark red, July–September, height 50 cm (1.64')	5?
'Jan's Wedding'	an unusually hardy yellow rose, height 1 m (3.25')	5
'Jens Munk'	Ex, *Rosa rugosa*, pink, somwhat full, continuous bloom	6
'John Cabot'	Ex, pinkish red, climber/shrub rose	5
'John Davis'	Ex, light pink double to half full flower, climber/shrub rose	5–7
'J. P. Connell'	Interesting variety but slow starter; takes a few years to become remontant; flowers in creamy white to yellow in July; sparsely remontant in fall, height 1–1.5 m (3.25'–5') This variety is from Ottawa.	5–6
'Louis Bugnet'	Elegant *Rosa rugosa* with reddish white buds and white full flowers. Grows into a robust shrub about 1 m (3.25') in height. See picture, p. 83	6
'Marie Bugnet'	sibling variety with filled fragrant white flowers	5–6
'Therese Bugnet'	sibling variety with full pink flowers and red buds. Grey green foliage; few prickles and red canes, flower from July to fall	6
'Martin Frobisher'	Ex, *Rosa rugosa*, light pinkish white, half full, blooms the entire summer, sprawling shrub	5
'Morden Amorette'	P, red continuous bloom if withered flowers are removed	5–6
'Morden Blush'	P, light pink, continuous bloom throughout summer, height 50 cm to 1 m (1.64' to 3.25')	6–7
'Morden Cardinette'	P, double red, continuous through summer, groundcover	5–6
'Morden Centennial'	P, pure pink, somewhat filled flowers, continuous bloom if withered flowers are removed	5–6
'Morden Fireglow'	P, scarlet red, not quite continuous bloom, height 0.5 to 0.7 m (1.64' to 2.30')	5–6
'Morden Ruby'	P, ruby red rose, sometimes some white spots, remontant, height 1 m (3.25')	6–7?
'Morden Snowbeauty'	P, the first white rose from Morden, low-growing groundcover with white, full, fragrant flowers	5?
'Morden Sunrise'	P, Morden's first yellow rose, fragrant yellow-orange, semi-double flower that opens completely; continuous bloom	5?
'Prairie Dawn'	double pink flower, a returning older variety (was sold at Bergianska trädgården—Bergianska Garden, Sweden—in early 1970s but its listing is missing from catalogues from the period)	4–5
'Prairie Joy'	light pink, a very resilient and hardy old variety, flowers profusely in June–July with sparse remontant fall flowers	6–7
'Sweet Adeline'	*Rosa rugosa* with pink full flowers, repeater	5–6
'Winnipeg Parks'	P, red ground cover rose, continuous bloom	5–6

Specific marketing groups

During the last few years we have begun to equate Canadian roses with hardy roses, but it isn't a group in its own right. Many of the roses are related to *Rosa rugosa* and show its typical wrinkled foliage, while others look more like common bedding roses. Most of them need to be cultivated in a colder climate and haven't yet proven successful in the south of Sweden. They're often afflicted with black spot and powdery mildew, diseases that pose no problem in northern Sweden. Some varieties aren't new. They existed before but disappeared due to lack of interest; they've now been re-established because there's a brand name that they can fit under.

Meanwhile, more interest is being shown in Finnish varieties. There's ongoing collaboration between northern Swedish and Finnish breeders to uncover hardy varieties, since the north of Sweden has more in common with Finland and the Torne Valley than with the Swedish and Danish plant institutes located farther south. In Finland, certain local specimens are collected and propagated—the *Rosa majalis* 'Foecundissima' for instance, known as the double cinnamon rose. In Sweden they're also hard at work breeding hardy and healthy roses—albeit on a smaller scale—at the Swedish agricultural college where the varieties 'Anna' (see picture on p. 82), 'Balder' and 'Irma' were launched.

Hardy Canadian roses

Canadian roses are typically available on the market on own stock, which is their main selling point. Most roses aren't grown this way but when they are, they're called 'own-root'. It has been argued that own-roots are hardier than other roses, but there isn't enough conclusive evidence to back up that assertion. (See 'Roses in garden centers and in cultivation,' p. 142.) Canadian roses are grouped into several series. The Explorer series, Ex, is *Rosa rugosas* or varieties where rugosas were used in the breeding, and varieties with Kordesi roses. *Rosa rugosas* are touted as resilient to salt, being healthy, hardy, and blooming more or less abundantly through the summer. Hybrids with Kordesi roses are usually lower growing climbing roses; they're bred in the Quebec area.

The Parkland series, P, is a line that includes the American *Rosa setigera*—the Michigan or prairie rose. These varieties are smaller, and might perhaps be hardier. They're bred at the Morden research facility in Manitoba on the Canadian prairie. Other varieties are issued from Canada but are not a part of these two series. The information passed on here about their size and flowering is applicable to the north of Sweden.

A vigorously growing Rosa rugosa—*probably 'Hansa'— is both hardy and a prolific bloomer. Here it grows with a guelder rose, also called European cranberry bush.*

Pruning modern shrub roses

As a group, 'modern shrub roses' is rather indistinct; consequently, it's not easy to know what's what. As such, it doesn't really matter, as long as the rose grows healthy. When it comes to pruning it, however, it's important to know what type of rose you're dealing with, so when purchasing the rose try to remember its given name, not just its variety. A modern shrub rose is not going to grow into a big shrub, but it can flower on both last year's and this summer's new growth, which is why you shouldn't cut it back too much.

Remove dead, damaged, and dry canes (also called diebacks); if there are a lot of small canes around the base, some of those can be taken off too. The shrub's height is evened out, and really long canes can be shortened if necessary. Older bushes can be thinned out a little, and one or a few older canes can be cut off at the base.

Modern shrub roses that flower on both this and last year's growth might not be hardy further north. They won't die but the canes will freeze—no canes will overwinter and form a shrub. The plant has to start all over every spring, and it might be lovely in a flowerbed but it will never become a large shrub.

Pruning shrub roses

Park and shrub roses grow significantly larger and sturdier than modern shrub roses. Large shrub roses can be compared to ornamental shrubs such as mock orange and lilacs. They're pruned by removing some of the older canes each spring—the canes are cut or sawn off at 5 to 10 cm (2" to 4") from the ground. The oldest canes turn grey and coarse; they often lack prickles, or have grey ones. Roses bloom most abundantly on new canes, so canes that are five to seven years old don't foster the same floral splendor and should therefore be removed.

Shrubs need many new young canes to replace the older ones that have been taken off, so leave the shoots growing around the plant alone. Trim them to the same height as the rest of the shrub. If you leave the shrub to grow tall and arching, it will shadow the ground beneath the shrub and no new shoots will be able grow there; the shrub will take on a 'vase' shape and will grow very few new flowers. When you thin out a few canes in the spring, remove the tallest ones—they cast the most shadow by arching out over the sides. You can cut them down to a third or fourth in length if there are many high canes arching outwards.

Rose hedges

Sturdy shrub roses can be grown as hedges. The roses are planted in a row like other hedge plants, and are pruned

A pruned shrub rose with a cloth weed barrier around its base. The oldest canes are pruned out to make room for new shoots.

at the same time as the planting. Bare-root roses are usually used for hedges (see 'Roses in garden centers and in cultivation,' p. 138) and they should only be planted in early spring or late fall.

If you want a straight lined hedge you'll have to prune the plants regularly each spring, and trim them a little in the summer also. A harder pruning is often done in early spring in order to not bother the plants again; if the plants are pruned in the summer, both decorative hips and new flower buds will be lost in the process.

At pruning time, do as you would for shrub roses: choose a few of the oldest canes and saw them off at about 5 to 10 cm (2" to 4") from the ground, that way room is freed up for new shoots to grow from the base to make the hedge denser. Young canes emerging in the summer tend to grow straight up, like arrows; you should shorten these a little to help them grow side shoots. If you don't thin out older canes, you'll eventually end up with a hedge that's bald at the base and with a very scant bloom.

Shrub roses can sometimes get a bit bare at the base. Prune them to ensure that new shoots emerge instead of old, non-productive canes left in year after year. While you're at it, add companion plants that will flower and fill in the gaps between the roses. Yellow spotted loosestrife and cranesbill look lovely together with the dark mauve 'Zigeunerknabe'—a rose variety still found in many older Swedish gardens.

If you neglect a hedge completely, you'll probably wind up with a tall, wide and straggly wall that will, in time, arch outward and keep spreading wider. It will splay open in the middle, weeds will take over, and there will be no new growth. If the hedge is that far gone, the only recourse is to prune it all the way down to 15 to 20 cm (6" to 8") above the ground, and hope it will have enough strength left to send out new, healthy shoots. These shoots will need to be pruned far down and thinned out to become a reasonably dense hedge. *Rosa rugosas* can handle that kind of rough treatment, and are very commonly used for hedges. Some burnet roses are even shaped this way.

Something to keep in mind is that these roses send up own-root shoots, and spread sideways; a hedge can be demanding of space if it isn't tamed. You must therefore prune and trim it, not only in height but also in width. Mark its allotted space and use the lawn mower to mow down any shoots that poke out in the lawn.

Sturdier bush roses can be planted together with clematis. Select varieties that bloom before, with, and after the rose—there are countless options. Here, shrub rose 'Frühlingsgold' is planted with clematis 'Yukiokoshi'.

Natural charm

Many charming plants that propagate by seed are suitable companions for shrub roses. While they might overrun a flowerbed or spread too freely, they get more competition with shrub roses. Digitalis, dusty miller, mullein, willow bell, and sweet William are all examples of such plants. They form upright spires, their flowers dot the sides of the stalks or are clustered at the top, while leaves form rosettes at the base. They're an excellent option since their leaves keep the weeds in check. Vigorous perennials such as spotted loosestrife, giant goldenrod, garden phlox and New York aster can also be used in companion plantings, although they will need a bit more nutrition and will make higher demands on the soil than the more resilient shrub roses. But if you fertilize in spring with long-acting fertilizer, and water the flowers as needed, the shrub roses will do well anyway. Both spotted loosestrife and giant goldenrod have a tendency to spread far and wide, but they're easily yanked up along with their roots if it gets too crowded.

Columbine is also an excellent companion plant. It flowers before the roses open, with slim elegant flower stalks above small tufts of leaves. If you choose a common columbine and leave the withered flowers alone, they will spread by seed. Many small plants will eventually cover the entire area beneath the roses.

Letting flowers propagate through self-seeding produces a charming and naturalistic cottage garden effect. The seeds germinate where it suits them, which can transform the look of the flowerbed from year to year as there are more and more plants growing. The roses grow in tandem, and in so doing shadow more and more of the ground. When the shrubs become large there won't be many plants between them—there'll be too much shade for them to grow. But on the outside in the sun the flowers will make an attractive border.

You can also introduce more subdued groundcovering plants. Since roses are sturdy, the area below them becomes shady and dry; while there aren't many plants that take well to drought and shade, bergenia, cranesbill, alpine bistort and bishop's hat are worth trying. Also, more traditional groundcovers such as lamb's ear, catsfoot and artemisia work well at the edge of shrub roses, where it's sunny and sometimes arid.

Not many shrub roses, with the exception of the *Rosa albas*, like to grow in more shadowy and damp areas, where they could be in the company of sweet woodruff. Sweet woodruff has a lovely scent and is a beautiful groundcover featuring fresh green leaves and white flowers. If you want to give it a try in a drier environment, however, you'll need to water it regularly if you expect it to thrive.

Companion plants with shrub roses

Sturdy shrub roses are suitable for companion planting with other plants. Non-repeating roses can become bare towards the base, which can start to look a bit lifeless once the flowers are spent and the rose hips and fall colors are still a way off. Their growth habit is more robust than bedding roses, so they can be planted with larger perennials; they're big enough to cope with a bit of competition from other plants. A peculiarity of the shrub rose is that you can let other plants climb onto it without the rose being harmed. Once burnet roses are done blooming in early summer, for instance, climbers such

Early spring finds the rose corner empty and lackluster. The birch tree needs a lot of water and nutrients, but in spring it's damp enough to allow for early tulips.

Later, the rose corner is in bloom and the spent foliage of the tulip is concealed. Meanwhile, columbines are showing off their color as they poke their heads up between the rose canes.

as clematis, nasturtiums, sweet peas, and morning glory can climb up and take over the flowering.

Annual climbers need a lot of water and nutrients to grow quickly, to become full and flower abundantly. One way to accommodate them is to place big pots of climbers next to the shrub rose and direct them towards the rose; that way the climbers get all the water and nutrition they need without running the risk of having to cede all their resources to the rose.

If clematis is set beside a shrub rose, it'll need to have a root barrier put in at the time of planting, like climbing roses that tend to grow up into other, more established plants (see description on p. 72). It's easy to lead clematis into a shrub rose because it attaches itself to the rose by way of its leaf tendrils.

Spring bulbs

Shrub roses are even compatible with spring flowering bulbs. When roses bloom they cast a shadow on the ground, but their companion bulbs have had time to flower beforehand. The bulbs benefit from the sun and light in spring, and then wilt in the shadow of the roses as they start to grow. Bulbs can take care of themselves; nevertheless it's a good idea, for both bulbs and roses, to fertilize in early spring. Spread the fertilizer lightly into the ground with a rake while at the same time removing some early weeds (see p. 100 for care of bulb beds and examples of bulbs). Small bulbs—even tulips—will become naturalized and spread in a loose setting, or in a spot where you want your garden to look more free form. Both woodland tulips and tarda tulips will happily self-seed given enough time. Late blooming Sprenger's tulips, with their bright red flowers, are also an awe-inspiring sight.

Summer blossoms in a rose corner situated near the sea and under a birch tree. These can be challenging conditions for the plants, but many varieties of burnet and Rosa rugosas *can handle this situation with aplomb. It's impossible to set up a traditional rose bed with perennials in this location, as the birch draws up all the available water and nutrients—even when the area gets supplemental irrigation. Burnet roses, however, can cope with dry and nutrient-poor soil, provide some protection from the wind, and—even though not as liberally as a bedding rose—still blooms. The foliage turns yellow in fall, sets attractive rose hips, and some of the roses even bring out a flower or two. Stonecrop is a great edging plant because it's drought-resistant and adds a rim of color to the sides of the flowerbed.*

A lovely and easy-to-care flowerbed featuring the groundcover rose, 'White Cover' and lavender. The soil must be weed-free at the time of planting to stay low maintenance.

ROSES THE EASY WAY

Many assume that roses are finicky and difficult to care for. By covering the ground with fabric or plants (or both), however, you can create a rose bed that's low maintenance. Roses can be planted on slopes and other larger surfaces without much trouble, too, once all the weeds have been removed.

During the middle and latter part of the 1900s, it was common to see long lines of tidy roses, standing as if on parade, on a flowerbed's bare earth. The soil between the roses was weeded and broken up—everything made to look spotless—on a weekly basis, something that few of us have the time or inclination for today. Besides, those gardens now look drab and uninspired; the flowers seem bare and exposed.

In old-world gardens with roses, medicinal plants, and herbs, roses were also kept in their own flowerbeds but were often surrounded by a hedge. The ground was covered with colored materials such as decorative gravel, seashells, crushed brick, or coal; all imparted a nice touch of color and hid the soil.

Easy care roses for flowerbeds

Today we can easily combine the effect of an old-fashioned rose garden with a more carefree lifestyle. The possibilities are endless, so your desires and preferences will ultimately steer you in the best direction. You can cover the ground for an easy, uniform appearance; while the flowerbed looks well tended throughout the year, at the peak of summer all the roses in bloom make it absolutely spectacular. Instead of spreading materials such as stone or mulch, you can use low-growing, spreading plants that are decorative for a good stretch of the year.

A paved stone path runs through larger shrub roses. Mass plantings on the ground, especially of cranesbill, become lush and care free. There's far less room for weeds; the few that might be there are more difficult to detect.

Cover the ground

You hardly ever see completely bare ground in nature—it's always covered in plants or plant debris. It's not good for the ground to be uncovered, as the sun scorches the surface, which then dries up and hardens. The soil needs to be broken up and loose before being irrigated to allow the water to seep in, otherwise a lot of water simply evaporates from the surface of the bare ground. So if you imitate nature and cover the ground, you'll be doubly rewarded: you'll avoid weeding, and the quality of the soil will improve.

There are several ways to cover the ground to prevent weeds from sprouting. Some weeds spread only through seeds, while others use both seeds and roots. Seeds on the ground need sunlight to germinate and grow; they die pretty quickly after germination if they don't get it. Weeds with strong roots like ground elder (also called bishop's weed) or couch grass also die if the leaves are covered and don't have access to light. To shield the weed from light, you can cover the ground with materials such as wood chips and gravel, black weed barrier fabric, a combination of black weed barrier fabric covered with other materials, or else with other plants. Cover plants will strangle seeds and roots after they develop and become established. Before planting a groundcover, you will have to start by covering the ground with fabric to kill off all existing weeds.

Here the ground has been covered in fabric for several years to allow the rose to develop. All weeds die off, but the process does take at least one full year.

Time to cover

If the ground is covered for one year, many of the weeds will be killed off. After that, you can remove the cover material and plant in that area, which will remain fairly weed-free and simple to care for if it's cleared when new weeds emerge. The drawback is that you have to wait a full year before planting anything in that spot.

Another option is to cover the ground with landscape fabric, cut holes in the fabric and plant roses through them. Weeds poking through the holes must be removed. The advantage of this method is that you can plant flowers straight away and gain a full year's worth of growth. The cover fabric stays on the ground and continues to kill the remaining weed seeds on the ground; you avoid all weeding except to take care of what comes through in the planting holes.

You can also use a combination of the two methods. Place the weed barrier fabric on the ground, make the holes, and plant the roses. The fabric then stays on the ground for two to three years to give the roses enough time to take root and develop, after which it is cut away; by this time hopefully the roses should be dense enough to cover the ground. You can also use companion plants as groundcovers, or spring bulbs for early flowers. This method saves a lot of effort and works as well with shrub roses.

Cover material

The material you use to cover the ground must not let any light through. Select material with a weave, or a fabric that breathes, to prevent the buildup of moisture under the cover. A plastic tarp or garbage bag is not a good option here, as rainwater stays on the impermeable surface of the cover and doesn't reach the roses. Mypex is a better choice: it's a groundcover made of woven black fabric that's sold in precut sheets, but can also be purchased in bulk. Landscape fabrics come in different thicknesses and some are UV resistant, a feature that will be reflected in the price (UV resistance means that the material is longer lasting because it won't break down from exposure to the sun's UV rays). Plantex UV resistant fabric is supposed to last thirty years. If you opt to use a non-UV-resistant cloth, you'll need to cover it with mulch or some other material.

Once the fabric is in place, go ahead and plant the roses. Make two small cuts in the cloth to form a '+' sign, then fold back the four flaps and dig a planting hole. After planting the rose, replace the flaps. In windy areas, secure the flaps with tent pins or place a stone on top. The outer edge of the fabric cloth should be dug down into the ground.

Decorative cover

After planting the flowers, you can cover the fabric with some other material such as bark mulch, wood chips, or cacao mulch; you can also put down a layer of gravel. All have their own particular advantages and disadvantages. The biggest drawback is that if the fabric is covered by a thick, protective layer, it will end up insulating the ground. This is good in winter, but it hinders the reheating of the ground in the springtime sunshine, thus holding the roses back from growing shoots and beginning to flower.

You can cover ground fabric with gravel, crushed brick, seashells, and other materials, as was described earlier in this section. In the past, different colored materials were used—red crushed brick, white limestone, black coal, as well as sand and gravel. In fact, any material that was

handy, as shown in Tycho Brahe's garden on the island of Hven in the 1500s, where they used crushed bluish black mussel shells.

If the fabric is covered with gravel or crushed brick, it will remain unchanged over many years (please note that it's not advisable to place gravel directly on the ground; without a sheet of fabric in between, the gravel might sink into the soil). The good thing about using gravel instead of other materials is that when the sun shines the gravel absorbs the heat, and disseminates it during the night when the ambient air is colder; this evens out the climate and temperature around the roses.

Modern roses in an old-world styled setting. Stones cover the ground around the roses, which are surrounded by a small brick ledge that is covered in plants. It looks just like a small hedge.

Cover material that requires fertilizer

Another option is to cover the ground with a layer of material thick enough that weeds can't penetrate it. Groundcover bark and wood chips are commonly used for this because they contain weed inhibitors. Covering the ground with bark mulch and wood chips does require extra care, though; since they're both natural products, they will eventually break down and molder. A lot of nutrients are needed for this decay to take place, and these are leached from the soil. None, or at least very little, nutrition is then left over for the roses, and if there is competition for nutrition, the bark mulch will always come out ahead. You will therefore need to fertilize your roses regularly, and in extra quantities. The more the mulch bark disintegrates, the more like earth it becomes. If you decide to forgo using a fabric cover, you'll need to set down a thick layer of bark mulch, which will cause the roses to get a later start in spring. If you do use fabric underneath the layer of bark mulch, then the layer needn't be so thick, but then you'll still need to apply extra fertilizer.

Cacao mulch has only recently been made available in Sweden. This mulch breaks down in the same way as wood chips. It's a byproduct of processing cacao beans, and consists of the thin shells from the beans. The shells contain substances that make the material bind into a hard

Mulch from cacao bean shells is a modern groundcover. However, extra fertilizing is needed so the roses can grow and develop properly.

crust. It stays put even on a slope, and doesn't blow away when dried out. Cacao mulch darkens with age, and ends up looking like soil—very dark brown in color. You can add cacao mulch in the fall to protect the plants from the winter cold, but even cacao mulch needs extra fertilizing.

Using cover plants against weeds

Another way to keep weeds down is to cover the ground under the roses with plants; this requires that the soil be weed-free before planting. Unfortunately, there are no chemicals that can be poured on the soil to kill all the weeds in the ground; and you can't just plant flowers in weedy soil, add bark mulch, and hope that the weeds will simply disappear. You will have to pull weeds repeatedly to remove all the weed roots and seed plants, and you'll need to weed regularly until the groundcover plants blanket the entire designated area. Weeds are weeds because they're very resilient and can grow just about anywhere. Weeding is a tedious chore, and a practical way to avoid it is to cover the ground with fabric first—see above. Cover the ground under the roses before planting them; leave the cover on for a year, then remove it and put in some groundcover plants. This will reduce your workload substantially, even if it does take longer before you can actually set anything in the ground.

Your best bets are low spreading plants that cover the ground and provide a beautiful backdrop for the rose foliage and blooms. Select plants that flower before the roses so your blooms last longer. Decorative leafy plants whose colors complement the rose are beautiful, even if they don't flower. Groundcovers prefer a sunny location, are drought tolerant, and grow quite densely. They don't

grow too tall or climb into the rose and choke it with a vigorous growth.

Many carpet-like groundcover plants have shallow roots or branches that trail along the ground. They're easy to pull up, which should be done in early spring; that clears off some soil near the rose canes, which is beneficial for the rose because it can then send out new shoots after it has been pruned, and suffers no competition from the groundcover plants. The groundcover fills in over the summer, leaving no room for weeds.

It's better to plant many small groundcover plants than fewer, large ones, so either buy many small plants or divide some larger ones. Some plants can also be grown from seed, which is a cost-effective way to get a large supply of plants. The more plants you set in the ground, the lovelier your flowerbed will look, and the quicker the ground will be covered.

Early flowering groundcovers

There are many plants that can act both as groundcover and as showy flowers. Early flowering plants are more rewarding, since roses come into bloom quite late. The following suggested flowers are predictable performers and all are excellent from spring to fall. They provide a beautiful carpet of foliage when flowering is over.

Catsfoot is a groundcover plant best suited for sunny and dry locations. Its foliage is greyish white and fuzzy with light to darker pink flowers, and looks uncannily like cats' paws. Wild (Alpine) strawberries are excellent for edging, but also work well as a groundcover. Growth habit can consist of sending out runners like Swedish 'Snövit' (Snow White) or 'Rödluvan' (Little Red Riding Hood) while others grow in a compact mound. Plants with runners send out long threads with small plants growing at the end, which then take root wherever they touch the soil. Alpine strawberries are easy to care for and produce lots of sweet berries. 'Pink Panda' and 'Lipstick' are fun hybrids of strawberries and shrubby cinquefoil—they grow like strawberries and alpines, send out runners and produce edible berries; the attractive and intensely bright pink flowers are slightly bigger than the ones on wild strawberries. They make superb groundcovers but can spread aggressively if they take well to the location. Creeping forget-me-not is also a lovely spring flowering groundcover. It's among the first garden perennials to show green, sending up leaf cones that later fold outward to cover the ground. The flowers are small—much like forget-me-nots—and bright blue; they do well in clay-like soil. Many of the plants commonly known as stonecrops produce mats of flowers, and can also be planted and used as such under roses.

Snow-in-summer, which is white and lights up the flowerbed in spring, is traditionally used as an edging plant. Its light silver-grey foliage is beautiful when paired with roses, which often have dark reddish green leaves when they leaf out. Tulip leaves disappear among other plants and are not very noticeable once roses start getting their foliage.

Underplantings for roses

Groundcover plants suitable to plant together with roses.

Catsfoot, *Antennaria*, unusual but very fitting, with silvery grey foliage.

Mountain rock cress, *Arabis*, usually produces white flowers

Wormwood, *Artemisia*, exists in both low-growing and tall varieties.

Artemisia, *Artemisia schmidtiana* 'Nana', silver grey and low growing.

Aubrietia, *Aubrietia*, bluish violet and reddish purple flowers, evergreen.

Campanula, *Campanula*, low-growing types like Dalmatian bellflower or Serbian bellflower can provide exquisite carpets of lovely blue flowers.

Snow-in-summer, *Cerastium tomentosum* group, an old-fashioned silver-grey edging plant.

Wild (alpine) strawberries, *Fragaria*, covers the ground with runners.

Sweet woodruff, *Galium odoratum*, white fragrant flowers that prefer a more shaded location.

Cranesbill, *Geranium*, many to choose from, like **bloody cranesbill** 'Album', 'Max Frei' and **ashy cranesbill** 'Purple Pillow', which thrive in a sunny and dry spot.

Moneywort, *Lysimachia nummularia*, luminous yellow flowers in early summer; can become invasive.

Creeping forget-me-not, *Omphalodes verna*, small bright blue flowers in early spring.

Moss phlox, *Phlox subulata*, exists in pinkish red shades, white, and pale blue. Flowers early.

Rockfoil, *Saxifraga*, rock garden plants in white or pinkish red; several different varieties exist.

Lambs' ear, *Stachys byzantina*, can rot if the winter is damp, but otherwise provides good coverage with nice grey downy foliage.

Thyme, *Thymus*, available in several varieties; Wooly thyme is elegant in a milder climate, but so is the hardier creeping thyme.

Lemon thyme, *Thymus x citroidorus*, grows decorative and lemon fragrant glossy green leaves almost year round.

The ground is covered in purple gromwell, pink rockrose, and pale grey lambs' ear.

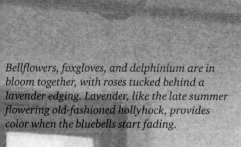

ROSES AND THEIR BEAUTIFUL COMPANIONS

Roses don't have to be kept apart from other flowers—by all means, group them with other plants. Companion planting will produce a delightful, long-lasting flower display, even in a small garden.

Bellflowers, foxgloves, and delphinium are in bloom together, with roses tucked behind a lavender edging. Lavender, like the late summer flowering old-fashioned hollyhock, provides color when the bluebells start fading.

An old-fashioned flowerbed (containing perennials such as goat's beard and peonies) flowers in the early summer. The roses start blooming as well, but will really come into their full glory in a few weeks' time when the peonies are spent.

Mixing many plants in the flowerbed provides flowers before, during, and after the blooming of roses. Weeds will have a hard time finding space to grow among all the flowers. Pests will become confused and find it difficult to settle in all the different plants.

If you mix different types of roses together, you'll prolong the blooming period. You often only have the choice between old-fashioned and modern roses. Many old-world, non-repeating roses are very elegant, and flower quite early in the season. If you plant these in the background, you can place continuously blooming varieties up front. Combine meter-high (3') shrubs with 60 to 70 cm (2') bedding roses; plant groundcover roses in front of them for a finishing touch.

By putting in a lot of different varieties you can have it all: heady fragrance, a multitude of vibrant colors, delightful rosehips, early flowers, wonderful fall colors, and an abundance of beautiful blooms through the entire summer. Climbing roses make a spectacular backdrop for bedding roses in matching or contrasting colors. There are so many options you may have trouble choosing among all the beautiful plants. Aside from combining different varieties of roses, stretch the flowering season by using other plants as companions. Select plants that will provide color and shape when they'll be appreciated the most. For example, summer flowers can star in the garden of a summer cottage, whereas early flowers followed by fall blooming perennials might be a more satisfying choice for a villa's garden.

'Golden Apeldoorn' is a tulip that comes back reliably each spring.

Bulbs as companion plants for roses

Grecian windflower, *Anemone blanda*, a white, pink, blueish-purple anemone with glossy flowers.

Glory-of-the-snow, *Chionodoxa forbesii*, white, blue, and pink tones, excellent for naturalizing.

Crocus, *Crocus*, many different varieties with flowers in yellow, purple, and white colors.

Winter aconite, *Eranthis hyemalis*, yellow; early flowering, excellent for naturalizing.

Snowdrop, *Galanthus nivalis*, white and elegant when planted in clusters.

Grape hyacinth, *Muscari*, blue and white varieties, easy to naturalize; grows in little mounds.

Striped squill, *Puschkinia scilloides*, white/light blue, with a striped flower.

Siberian squill, *Scilla siberica*, bright blue, common, grows low to the ground like a mat.

Tulip, *Tulipa*, exist many colors except bright blue; from early-flowering single flower to later, fuller, peony-like varieties.

Tulipa species (wild or dwarf tulips) such as the **peacock tulip** from the *Tulipa greigii* group, most commonly found in yellow, red, and white; and some are also orange and pink. Many have beautifully patterned petals.

'Shirley' is an excellent tulip that pairs well with young, reddish-green rose foliage.

Early spring with bulbs

The onset of spring is the right time for bulbs to shine in the rose bed. Many gardeners favor the first spring flowers over all other plants because they are the first to appear after the long cold season. Early spring bulbs are small and short-stemmed, and don't take up a lot of space between the roses while still providing great bursts of color. If you prefer tidy flowerbeds, opt for bulbs that grow in clusters or mounds, like snowdrops and grape hyacinths. However, small bulbs like Siberian squill and glory-of-the-snow are best spread under large shrub roses, as they can look a bit messy when they pop up all over the flowerbed.

The earliest bulbs to flower are the snowdrop, winter aconite and grape hyacinth, and all enjoy the company of roses. Crocuses appear a bit later, but put on a no less impressive show in various shades of mauve, yellow, and white. Later to flower still are the short-stemmed *Tulipa* species in shades of red, orange, and yellow; their foliage doesn't poke up between the rose canes in June, all brown and withered, but instead settle on the ground below the roses and waste away out of sight. If you fertilize and water the tulips during and after flowering, they'll happily return year after year, and might even multiply. Roses reap the benefit of being fertilized early in the season, which makes *Tulipa* species perfect companion plants. *Narcissus*, i.e. easter and Whitsun lilies, prefer damper soil and probably wouldn't thrive quite as well as tulips, but try them anyway—if they're happy they'll quickly grow into sturdy clusters.

DEER-RESISTANT BULBS

An added bonus to not pruning your roses too early in the season is that deer will leave your tulips alone. Never mind how tempting budding tulips are, deer prefer not to stick their muzzles into the prickly rose canes. Botanical tulips—*Tulipa* species—are shorter-stemmed, and their leaves are typically bunched near the ground. Once in flower these tulips aren't very tasty to deer, so it doesn't matter if they reach up above the canes.

Spring splendor in a sunny corner, with a view of flowering bulbs and a cherry tree. Red and yellow roses put on a beautiful display once the tulips have withered.

The care of rose bed with bulbs

A rose bed planted with bulbs doesn't require a lot of care; quite the opposite—it's better to leave it alone. Fertilize it early in spring when the bulbs begin to flower; snip off any withered flowers, but let the foliage grow undisturbed. Their leaves will wither in summer; when they've dried out completely, go ahead and remove them.

To keep things simple, plant tall tulips to one side of the roses. Choose a space where the withered foliage can be concealed as much as possible from the garden, deck, or patio. In full bloom, tulips are still visible above the roses that have not yet opened.

Bulbs prefer a dry and sunny location in summer, so in order to encourage them to grow lively in the flowerbed, place a drip hose on the side of the roses away from the bulbs to irrigate the roses while avoiding the bulbs.

Bulbs are planted in the fall. They need to be set in as deeply as is possible without damaging the roses' root system. While smaller bulbs are easy to plant, tulip bulbs can be a bit trickier. Cover the flowerbed and the bulbs with plenty of soil; gather soil from the vegetable patch or another flowerbed in the garden and pile it on. The soil provides winter protection for the roses and covers the bulbs at the same time.

Grape hyacinths bloom even earlier than tulips; they multiply and spread year after year.

Aubrietia, an early flowering plant, covers the ground between the roses.

Roses with flowering perennials

Once the early bulbs' flowers are spent and the last big tulips have fully opened, roses begin to show foliage, but it's still too early for them to show a lot of color. Even roses that flower continuously through the summer don't start to bloom until the month of June, and even later if they're further up north. If you plant early blooming perennial flowers, the flowerbed will be full of color before your roses are in bloom. Choose different varieties, or perhaps just one mass planting of a single variety.

It's preferable to select plants that thrive in sunny and dry conditions, and avoid the ones best suited for part to full shade and damp soil. Roses need sunshine, and they take up a lot of water and nutrients from the soil, so try to find companion plants that can tolerate a drought. You don't want the filler flowers to monopolize the roses' sustenance and not make them look their best.

Many low-growing, spreading plants make fine edging plants. Moss phlox, aubrietia and snow-in-summer are commonly used both as groundcover and in borders. Cranesbill is slightly larger, so it can also be used as a groundcover or an edging plant. Most cranesbills flower early in summer and can re-bloom with a sprinkling of flowers later on in the season.

Spring flowers that re-bloom year after year

Primulas (including primroses) are in a large group of plants that flower in early spring. They come in many shapes and forms, from low growing, compact and resilient in a multitude of colors, to taller, more elegant varieties. Various types, like the English garden primrose, polyanthus primula (oxlip), and Himalayan (cowslip) primrose are excellent choices for early flowers. All form mounds and grow wider each year, bearing more and

more flowers. They're quite tough but need damp soil, which is a pretty common in spring. The hardiest and most commonly found example in the spring garden is 'Wanda', a primrose with a bright lilac flower and a yellow center.

Both primulas and primroses are popular houseplants, and can be easily transplanted into the garden after Easter when they're done flowering inside. Garden primroses are exceptionally hardy—they come back year after year and can even flower under the snow.

Aubrietia is another well-known edging plant that likes dry and sunny ground. It stays greenish grey year round and spreads like a mat. It flowers early in bright blue violet and is hardy up to Central Sweden.

The snowdrop anemone is an old-timer in the flowerbed, and is a white single flower that can be found bordering many an allotment flowerbed. The double-flowered kind is more elegant than the single flower, but it doesn't bloom as abundantly. Columbines are true charmers—albeit a bit old-fashioned—and early bloomers. They grow in round clusters and send up elegant thin flower stalks between the rose canes. They're a sturdy plant and are especially good matches for shrub roses. Leopard's bane is a very early bloomer and is very easy to grow. Its sun-yellow daisy-like flowers die down long before the roses start opening, but its foliage is a beautiful light green that makes a nice filler plant the rest of the summer.

Resilient and old-fashioned

Mountain bluet or cornflower is an old-fashioned perennial with quite a short flowering period. Most of the time it sits there inconspicuously, then it suddenly bursts into a most intensely purple blue flower—in fact, it's one of the bluest flowers around. This characteristic, along with being very hardy and easy to grow, makes it an excellent choice for tougher climates. Trim it all the way down after it's spent, and with any luck it might produce a second round of flowers. Knapweed looks very similar and can be found in very intense reddish purple shades.

Western bleeding heart is a minor relative of the bleeding heart. It has a long flowering period and covers the ground with mounds of greenish blue, finely lobed leaves. It isn't really suitable for growing with roses, but it is such a long-flowering plant that it might be worth trying out on the shadier side of the rose bed (it's usually recommended as groundcover for partly shaded areas of the yard). Bleeding heart can also be planted in the rose bed, as they come into flower before the roses begin to bloom, and then die down pretty quickly.

Cushion spurge makes for a bright splash of color in the rose bed. Not only does it feature small lime yellow flowers in early summer, but its bright lime yellow bracts continue to enhance the flowerbed over several more weeks. Plus, this plant is drought resistant and productive, with a pillow-forming growth habit. It spreads a lot over time and

Lady's mantle stays delicately yellowy green over a long time and pairs well with all different rose colors.

might need to be divided or sequestered. Cushion spurge looks good at the base of climbing roses and clematis. Lady's mantle is very resilient, and is another example of a plant with lime green flowers that stays attractive long after the flowers are gone. It's a very leafy plant that can grow large. It tolerates both shade and sun and can, in fact, almost turn into a bit of an invasive weed. A combination of lady's mantle and yellow roses, however, is a bold and delightful choice.

Roses and many different types of cranesbill look lovely together.

Early flowering perennials in the rose bed

Many early flowering perennials have low growing and spreading growth habits, so they can be used as groundcovers. Other early flowering perennials waste away quickly and make ample space for summer flowers.

Lady's mantle, *Alchemilla mallis*, a dependable and resilient plant.

Snowdrop windflower, *Anemone sylvestris*, old-fashioned with white flowers.

Columbine, *Aquilegia vulgaris*, there are many varieties in lots of colors, from blue and yellow to red and pink.

Mountain bluet, *Centaurea montana*, a classic plant in bright blue.

Western bleeding heart, *Dicentra formosa* group, flowers in soft pink on an attractive leafy mound.

Leopard's bane, *Doronicum orientale*, early blooming, bright yellow, daisy-like flowers

Cushion spurge, *Euphorbia polychroma*, bright lime green-yellow, long flower period

Cranesbill, *Geranium*, many different types and sizes

Spring vetch, *Lathyrus vernus*, quite uncommon, mauve or pink, tolerates drought well and blooms in neat little clusters

Giant poppy, *Papaver orientale* group, lovely colors and elegant buds, but withers quickly.

Primula, *Primula pruhoniciana* group, early flowers, an almost luminous violet.

Himalayan meadow primrose, *Primula rosea*, primrose with dainty pink, hint of red flowers.

Primrose, *Primula vulgaris*, can be found in many colors, blue to white, to pink, red and yellow.

Rockfoils, *Saxifraga*, blooms in white or pinkish red shades.

Primulas and primroses are vibrantly colored, resilient plants that flower over a long period in early spring.

Perennials that bloom together with roses

Yarrow, *Achillea millefolium*, can be found in pink, red, and orange, and also in muted pastel colors.

White tansy, *Achillea ptarmica* var. multiplex, ornamental sneezewort.

Giant hyssop, *Agastache*, its blue flowers are attractive to beneficial insects.

Pearly everlasting, *Anaphalis margaritacea*, has silver-grey leaves and bright yellow flowers.

Triple-nerved pearly everlasting, *Anaphalis triplinervis*, grey downy leaves, white flowers with yellow centers.

Snow carpet, *Anthemis carpatica*, a relative of yellow chamomile, with silver-grey leaves.

Calamint, *Calamintna nepeta* 'Blue Cloud', pale blue, almost white gossamer-like flower, fragrant leaves.

Bluebells, *Campanula*, many varieties and sizes with blue and white flowers.

Delphiniums (larkspur) *Delphinium*, in many blue and pink shades.

Maiden pink, *Dianthus deltoides*, drought tolerant, bright red, also in white and pink.

Cheddar pink, *Dianthus gratianopolitanus*, small soft pink flowers.

Pinks, *Dianthus plumarius*, fine petal elegant flowers.

Baby's breath, *Gypsophila paniculata*, gossamer-like white bloom, good for drying.

Hyssop, *Hyssopus officinalis*, bright blue flowers.

Knautia, *Knautia macedonica*, dark wine red. Typically needs support from neighboring plants.

Lavender, *Lavandula angusitfolia*, classic lilac edging and border plant.

Shasta daisy, *Leucanthemum*, white, full flower.

Catchfly, *Lychnis coronaria*, silver leaves with magenta-red flowers, spreads through seed.

Garden catmint, *Nepeta x faassenii*, traditional silver-blue edging plant.

Woodland sage, *Salvia nemorosa*, many fine blue-violet versions good for mixing.

Mullein, *Verbascum*, tall, slim flower spires, blooms in pink, yellow-orange, and purple shades.

Rosa 'Yellow Submarine' planted together with catchfly.

Fashionable cranesbill

There are many varieties and colors of cranesbill that pair well with roses. Flower colors range from white to blue, and reddish purple to lilac and pink. Their heights vary from the short ashy cranesbill to the tall meadow cranesbill. French—or Endress'—cranesbill feels right at home everywhere and spreads a bit too willingly, as does rock cranesbill. Nevertheless, some varieties of bloody cranesbill are low growing and worth planting. The quite recent 'Brookside' is a taller type, as is the well-known 'Johnson's Blue', which can be found in many older gardens. 'Rozanne' is also a new variety in bright bluish purple that flowers the entire summer, as does 'Jolly Bee'.

Purple cranesbill, often found in older gardens, puts on a lovely show of flowers in June, just before the roses open. The leaves of many cranesbills take on gorgeous fall colors, and they blanket the ground beneath the roses.

Blooming to perfection

Spring and early summer plants blossom *before* roses open. However, if your goal is to keep beautiful flowerbeds throughout the summer, then you'll have to pick plants that flower *simultaneously* with the roses to underscore their beauty. Tall, thin, airy spires that peek out from the rose canes are a truly wonderful sight. In a vintage volume about roses, the author, a rose grower and breeder, suggests planting Madonna lily, regal lily, and baby's breath between the roses to make a combination of white plants that doesn't dominate the roses, merely compliments them. Lilies have few leaves, same as baby's breath. Good companion plants should have leaves bunched at their base so they don't cover up the stars of the show.

The plants you choose as companion plants will depend on your personal preference, as well as on the color of the roses. They in their turn might have been selected to match the color of your house or other elements in the garden. A sense of unity and consistence is an essential factor in an attractive landscape, and winding filler plants provide this visual coherence in the garden. Winding plants are so named because they wind their way—their branches often light, airy, and sprinkled with small flowers—through other plants.

Perennials that you choose as companion plants for your roses will grow and spread each year, and will progressively fill the spaces between them. If there's a bare spot anywhere in the flowerbed, it's easy to fill it with annual summer flowers, which allows you to change up the look of the flowerbed whenever you like.

Company in silver and white

Roses look gorgeous paired with white and silver. As neutral colors, they help bring out the palette of the roses. Many silver-grey leaved plants are also very drought-resistant and keep well over a long period of time; however, many have vigorous growth habits and can spread aggressively if they like their spot. When weeding in spring, take the opportunity to dig up some of those more space-hungry plants.

White tansy is a dainty, flower-rich, and full variety of sneezewort. Its small white flowers and bright green leaves spread easily in the flowerbed, and it is very hardy.

With its silvery grey leaves and small clusters of yellow flowers, pearly everlasting stays decorative through the entire summer. It spreads far and wide in well-drained soil, so it

Blue larkspurs and brown accented red daylilies together with yellow, red, and pink roses.

White tansy, oxeye daisies as well as the silver-grey foliage of triple-nerved pearly everlasting all brighten the whiteness of the 'Little White Pet' rose.

Rosa 'Sophia Renaissance', together with the long lasting, lovely flowers of the bluish violet woodland sage. The sage flower still stays decorative after wilting. The variegated foliage of Indian aster picks up the yellow tint of the rose.

needs a firm, controlling hand. Triple-nerved pearly everlasting is a close relative of pearly everlasting, and is one of my favorite companion plants for roses. Its leaves are silvery grey-green and decorative in their own right. The flowers are small white balls collected in what looks like a little broom.

Calamint and large-flowered calamint are little-known plants for the flowerbed in Sweden, but both bloom over a long period and are productive. Calamint in particular does well in a sunny, dry location. It's a romantic and delicate companion plant.

There are many types of dianthus. Maiden pink, cheddar pink, and pinks are all varieties that seem to be hardy throughout most of Sweden. Carnations can be added to the list of capable flowers for the south of Sweden. Dianthus has slim grey-green leaves that are very pretty, even when the plant is not in flower. They work well in edgings and flower borders, and their delicate flowers impart a glow to the flowerbed. Maiden pink is hardy, and bears flowers in lovely colors. Many dianthus can be bought as summer bedding plants.

Baby's breath can be both an annual and a perennial plant. The perennial variety makes perfect companion plants for sturdy roses. The perennial baby's breath has a carrot-like root that's deeply anchored in the ground. It does take its own sweet time to grow—a year, maybe even two—but once it starts it is exceptionally lovely and is very drought tolerant. Baby's breath appears quite late in the season, leaving the flowerbed looking a bit forlorn, but when it blooms it stays handsome well into the fall. Creeping baby's breath has, as the name indicates, a creeping growth habit, as does the hybrid 'Rosenschleier'; they both feature either pink or white flowers.

Blue spires

Bluebells come in lots of guises: some are short-stemmed rock garden plants that grow in the shape of a floor mat, such as Dalmatian bellflower, diminutive bellflower (fairy thimbles) and tussock bellflower; others are uprights with undulating bells on delicate stalks, like the willow bell (also known as peach-leaved bellflower), or many small bells on a coarser stalk, like the milky bellflower. Whatever the variety, they all look stunning in a rose bed. The shorter-stemmed types are more drought-tolerant and flower quite early in the season. Upright, tall bellflowers that can multiply prefer a sturdier and damper soil. Pair willow bells with pink, white, and red roses for an incredibly romantic combination; willow bells and milky bellflowers, which spread quickly, can be well matched with sturdy shrub roses.

Delphiniums (larkspurs) are striking plants that grow so tall that they need added support, and protection from the wind, preferably next to a wall. They pair especially well with climbing roses. Delphiniums are typically blue and lilac. Bright blue Chinese delphiniums grow shorter than tall delphiniums

Woodland sage and bloody cranesbill thrive in the blazing hot sun, here together with a small goat willow, which continues to give shape to the planting even in wintertime. The rose is probably 'Sympathie', a common climber that grows well in the south of Sweden.

and can often manage without support; sadly, they don't last long but they still make fantastic companion plants.

Traditional edging

Lavender has been grown together with roses for centuries in herb gardens, since the time when roses were considered to be, amongst other things, medicinal plants. Lavender belongs with roses as no other plant does; it's a half shrub that overwinters with its branches aboveground, and is pruned each spring. Its leaves are green with a more or less pronounced grey shimmer, depending on variety. The flowers are typically purple, but they also come in white and pink. Lavender needs well-drained soil to be able to overwinter without problems.

Hyssop is also a member of the herb and medicinal plant family, and it usually bears blue flowers. As with lavender, there are some varieties that come with white or pink flowers, but they're of a more delicate nature. Its leaves are bright green, but its growth habit is reminiscent of the lavender. Hyssop is probably a bit hardier than lavender and can be used as a low hedge or as an edging plant around roses.

Woodland sage looks a little like lavender and hyssop, and is an old ornamental plant. The head of the flower retains its purple color even when the individual flower has withered. 'Caradonna' is an especially fine variety. Woodland sage is quite short-lived but it will self-seed if the seed heads aren't snipped off. Weed carefully in early spring so the small new leaf rosettes aren't inadvertently pulled out.

Aromatic herbs and foliage

Giant hyssop is a wonderfully aromatic herb that thrives in sun and heat. It's a perennial in the south of Sweden, while further north it can be transplanted out in spring. Its slim, tall bluish purple tubular flowers stay attractive for a long time, making it an excellent companion plant. Just like lavender, giant hyssop also attracts lots of butterflies and beneficial insects to the flowerbed.

Nepeta, commonly called garden catmint, features aromatic, silver-grey leaves and small blue flowers. Traditionally it's an edging plant, and is used in the same way as lavender, but garden catmint is hardier than lavender. The drawback to catmint is that it flattens down and becomes very wide; the good thing about it is that its leaves keep the plant looking beautiful for a long time. Other catmints like, say, *Nepeta nervosa,* have blue flowers and aromatic leaves and look very good when planted as companions in the rose bed. Another member of the mint family, oregano, also flowers beautifully and has very fragrant leaves. Oregano comes in many varieties—some more, some less spicy. Several new ones—'Herrenhausen,' for example—flower abundantly and are only used for ornamental purposes. 'Herrenhausen' attracts butterflies with its dark red-purple flowers, which are magnificent together with pink, white, and yellow roses.

Giant hyssop has scented aromatic leaves, and attracts butterflies and other beneficial insects. At the front is a lavender cotton plant that can be swapped out for wormwood or a hardy triple-nerved pearly everlasting in colder climates.

Colorful winding filler plants

Knautia is a filler plant that carries lots of button-like flowers on top of branching stems. These grow here and there, and aptly fill the spaces between the roses. Its color is quite unusual, a very deep red without a hint of lilac. Flowering starts out sparse and never becomes overwhelming; it simply continues to flower until late summer. Knautia favors sunny spots with well-drained soil, and will self-seed if it likes the location. Flowering will be more plentiful if the faded flowers are snipped off. Catchfly is a slightly older plant with purple-red flowers; its color is intense and contrasts sharply with the silver-grey leaves. It's a biennial that will self seed if the spent flowers are left on the stalks. It spreads charmingly in the flowerbed and never takes over, but is easily pulled up if it spreads too much (there's a white variety that doesn't spread as much). The soil needs to drain properly for its leaf rosettes to overwinter successfully.

Digitalis self seeds willingly, so leave it to spread freely among the shrub roses along with bellflowers and catchfly. Catchfly is an extremely likeable plant, but it can spread a bit too freely; see picture on p. 77.

Marguerite (or oxeye daisy) is the perfect complement to roses if you're creating a romantic, Swedish-themed flowerbed. Shasta daisies don't spread with quite such gusto as common daisies. There are many varieties of white daisies, tall and short stemmed, full or single flowered. Shasta daisies grow best in a sturdier, nutrient-rich soil.

Velvet plant (mullein) and purple mullein are changeable filler plants that bring an old-fashioned cottage appeal to the flowerbed. They can be found in apricot, pink and lilac shades. Mulleins will spread easily as soon as planted, but old plants die off just as quickly. If they like the location, they'll make surprise appearances every year, in a range of colors and in different spots from where they were originally planted.

Roses with annual summer flowers

Annuals as company in the rose bed are a popular and always beautiful sight. With their assistance, the garden can change color and feel, even though the roses stay the same. Richly colored summer flowers, following close on the heels of spring bulbs, can be planted among the roses and other plants where the bed needs filling in.

If you want to delight in a vibrantly colored flowerbed in spring, purchase flowering bedding plants and transplant them outside as soon as the risk of frosty nights has passed. For more unusual or exotic specimens, start them yourself in your house and transplant them later among the roses. The advantage of most summer flowers is that they, like roses, need plenty of water and nutrients, and thrive when obliged. Especially suited are summer flowers with finely lobed leaves and lots of small flowers; they fill in the space between the roses and surround them in lush green vegetation. Large-flowered plants with a single large flower, like dahlias, don't work as well because they tend to become focal points, drawing away instead of enhancing the loveliness of the roses.

Spring flowering bedding plants

Pansies and miniature pansies can be transplanted into the garden very early in spring. They can put up with some frost as long as they've been allowed to acclimatize for a few days first. Transplant them outside when the weather is mild and there's no longer any frost at night. If the weather unexpectedly turns chilly (which tends to happens in spring) the plants are hardened off and there's no harm done. They'll do fine down to about -5°C to -7°C (19°F to 23°F), even with some snow. They might look a bit creased but they'll soon perk up again. Miniature, or mini, pansies are especially hardy and flower willingly. Remove wilted flowers by hand and the bloom will last a long time. They will repeat bloom in summer if you cut them down in early summer; they'll come back once more as fall approaches. Early flowering forget-me-nots and primulas are other good plants to buy and set out among roses. When their blooms end other summer flowers take their place, but the pansies usually stay.

Blue summer flowers

Early summer sees the arrival of traditional summer flowers. They're demanding plants—just like roses—and will flower as long as they get plenty of water and nutrients, up until the first frost. Every year it's a pleasure and great fun to choose new varieties and colors of annuals. We Swedes love the color blue, and blue flowers happen to look lovely in the rose bed. Cut-leaf daisies form beautiful tufts that cover the ground beneath the roses. Bindweed is a more unusual plant— still blue—with funnel-shaped flowers. It looks like a small morning glory but it grows more like a pillow. Another blue blossom is the pretty laurentia, with its deeply segmented leaves; it grows into a lovely round mound. White roses paired with bright blue larkspurs are delightful, and petunias, which can be found in a multitude of colors and sizes, pair well with just about any flower.

Another way to combine annuals is by grouping different flowers in grades of blue. Mealycup sage with upright violet-blue flowers is pretty when planted alongside blue marguerite. Being vigorous growers, surfinia trailing petunia and scaveola—also called fairy fan-flower—can be difficult to grow in the rose bed. If you decide to try them, remember that they need copious amounts of water and nutrients but the result can be incredibly flower-rich and visually stunning.

Swan River daisy is a favorite among the bedding plants. It fills in very nicely between the roses with its narrow segmented leaves, and it flowers a long time in bluish purple. This daisy, like roses, needs plenty of water and nutrients to coax it into growing large and producing a lot of flowers.

Blue summer flowers

Swan River daisy, *Brachyscome iberidifolia*, low mounds.

Field larkspur, *Consolida*, is an annual variety of larkspur with a graceful growth habit.

Bindweed, *Convolvulus*, is an unusual edging plant.

Blue marguerite, *Felicia amelloides*, has dainty and long-flowering lilac blue blades.

Heliotrope, *Heliotropium*, dark violet and scented, slow growing.

Lobelia, *Lobelia erinus*, is a well-known edging plant.

Laurentia, *Laurentia axillaris*, pretty mild blue or pink.

Petunia, *Petunia x hybrida*, exists in a multitude of colors and combinations.

Trailing petunias, *Calibrachoa*, 'Million Bells' and 'Callie' are low spreading varieties with small, weather resistant flowers.

Mealycup sage, *Salvia farinacea*, deep violet-blue color.

Gentian sage, *Salvia patens*, is as blue as the sky.

Fan flower, *Scaevola*, a flower for hanging planters, with lilac flowers. A wide growth habit; even used as groundcover.

Pink summer flowers

Summer flowers will bloom even more generously if the faded flowers are removed, which is easy to do while you deadhead the roses.

Pinks, *Dianthus*, many varieties and forms, always features attractive grey-green foliage

Twinspur, *Diascia*, pinkish red, white and pale lilac shades.

Gaura, *Gaura lindheimeri*, small flowers in white or pink.

Petunia, *Petunia x hybrida*, exists in a multitude of colors and forms, just as the small-flowered versions.

Trailing petunias, *Calibrachoa*, series 'Million Bells', 'Callie' and others.

Verbena, also **vervain**, *Verbena*, in clear colors and also pastels; both have trailing and upright growth habits.

Marigold is an incredibly rewarding bedding plant that tolerates rain.

Yellow summer flowers

Fern-leaved beggarticks, *Bidens ferulifolia*, pillow-like growth.

Jamesbrittenia, *Jamesbrittenia*, one of the newer plant varieties for hanging planters.

Nemesia, *Nemesia*, exists in all hues and colors imaginable.

Creeping zinnia, *Sanvitalia procumbens*, has small and pointy yellow petals and spreading growth.

Marigold, *Tagetes*, exists in all imaginable brown, yellow and orange shades.

Signet marigold, *Tagetes tenuifolia*, great filler and long blooming.

Pink dreams

Pink is the most common color of rose, and there is a vast array of pink shades out there to discover. The same can be said for the color pink with regards to bedding plants. An easy combination of blue and pink blooms can certainly be replaced with fine-tuned, pink-only complimentary shades in the rose bed. It needn't involve only two colors, either; white roses can keep the company of both blue and pink bedding plants. Or, try something edgier by combining pink annuals with red roses, and accents of silver grey and purple leafy plants.

Twinspur is one of the best pink summer flowers for the garden. It's a newcomer to Sweden and is commonly seen in hanging baskets in sunny locations. Small, dainty flowers on slender stalks fit in nicely among the roses, and their leaves cover the ground. The flowers can be pink, lilac, or salmon orange. It's somewhat drought tolerant and blooms long into fall.

Dianthus, commonly called pinks, is a beauty traditionally seen in companion plantings with roses. It comes in pink, red, and white shades, and even in stronger colors. An extremely versatile bedding plant with varying growth habits, it can trail from hanging planters, but can also grow in pillow-like mounds. Include it as an edging plant or let it lean against the roses. Gaura is a new, totally charming and very popular filler plant. Its soft pink or white butterfly-like flowers sit high up on slender stalks.

Vibrantly orange

Yellow, red, and orange are strong colors that reflect brilliantly in sunshine. There are many bedding plants in shades of red to yellow, and yellow shifting into orange. Marigolds are one of the most popular examples, and they're often planted together with roses in flowerbeds. It's been said that planting marigolds among roses is good for the roses and for the soil, but that's only a part of the story. Some marigolds, and under specific conditions, can rid the soil of rose plant disorder; unfortunately, the ability of marigolds to scare off aphids is only an old wives' tale.

Be that as it may, we know marigolds are worthwhile companions as they're weather resilient and prolific bedding plants. They're hugely diverse: small flowers, large flowers, short-stemmed and tall, with flowers in all shades of yellow and orange with a hint of rusty red. Especially lovely is the variety of small, spice-scented signet marigold. Pretty and easy to cultivate, it grows in a plump pillow of finely textured leaves and is covered in flowers.

Fern-leaved beggarticks, with its fine and narrow leaves and bright yellow flowers, is hardy with a sprawling growth and a prolonged flowering period. Used in hanging baskets and planters, it's also a nice edging filler plant for rose beds, but it shouldn't be used with all roses due to its intense color. Creeping zinnia has small, spiky yellow flowers with a clearly visible center in brown or greenish yellow. Its spreading growth habit makes it an excellent edging plant. Jamesbrittenia, from South Africa, is another plant meant for the hanging planter. It thrives in full sun and will spread along the ground. The flowers come in different rust orange hues that can be very impactful in combination with white, yellow-orange, and pink roses.

Nemesia is one of the few plants truly available in all colors, from bright blue to yellow, pink and red. Several new varieties are bi-colored and make great fillers with their many small flowers.

American blue vervain, which, contrary to its name, comes in both blue and pink. There are many varieties of verbena, both upright and trailing, and they all like to be in a sunny spot.

Vibrantly colored leafy plants

Grey hair grass, *Corynephorus canescens*, steely blue dense clusters in a half-spherical shape.

Kidney weed, also **Asian ponysfoot**, *Dichondra michranta*, exists also in pure green.

Love grass, also Elliott's love, *Eragrostis elliotii*, 'Wind Dancer', blue-green foliage and plumes of white flowers. This grass is tall and needs quite a lot of space. Try it in a container placed next to the roses.

Showy baby's breath, *Gypsophila elegans*, white, gossamer-like flower.

Cushion baby's breath, *Gypsophila muralis*, green mound dotted with small spots of pinkish white flowers.

Licorice plant, *Helichrysum petiolare*, vigorous growing leafy plant with long shoots.

Foxtail barley, *Hordeum jubatum*, large, graceful glinting flower heads.

Sweet potato, *Ipomoea batatas*, is an interesting newcomer to Swedish bedding plants.

Pearl millet,'Purple Majesty', *Pennisetum americanum*, red-leafed. Large and demanding, but very beautiful.

Beefsteak plant, *Perilla frutescens*, nettle-like with leaves in dark red, or bicolor green and white.

Coleus, *Solenostemon scutellarioides*, old-fashioned houseplant that has now moved to the flowerbed.

Easy-to-grow flowers with roses

Satin flower, *Clarkia amoena*, there are many lovely new varieties in pink, red, and white shades.

Spider flower, *Cleome hassleriana*, tall to extremely tall, will need support.

Garden cosmos, also **Mexican aster**, *Cosmos bipinnatus*, comes in many shades of pink.

California poppy, *Eschscholzia californica*, silk thin petals in lovely shades, especially orange and fire red.

Rose mallow, *Lavatera trimestris*, bright and shiny flowers in pink or metallic white.

Livingstone daisy, *Mesembryanthemum*, unusual, but easy to grow and resilient; comes in many colors.

Love-in-a-mist, *Nigella damascena*, bright blue, lilac, or white with fennel-like foliage.

Opium poppy, *Papaver somniferum*, Peony Poppy group; absolutely wonderful and multi-hued, unfortunately its blooming period is too short.

Garden nasturtium, *Tropaeolum majus*, trailing or bush nasturtiums make lovely fillers around roses.

Vibrantly colored leafy plants

The current trend in Sweden is plants with colored foliage, which are eminently suitable as companion plants for roses. As the plants' lives span only over the summer, this allows us to be a bit more daring in trying them out; they're quick and easy to remove or change if they don't work out. Leafy plants, too, should be chosen with an eye on how they'll complement the color of the roses. If you want a cooling effect, go for silver. The licorice plant has silver-grey, lime-green, or variegated leaves. It's a vigorous grower with long branches that weave between the roses, and it looks lovely next to a rose with dark foliage such as 'H. C. Andersen'. Kidney weed, also known as Asian ponysfoot, grows flat along the ground and gives a different impression altogether. Its leaves are silvery green, matte, and very light-colored; the plant will eventually cover the ground (even if it takes its time in doing this) so this plant is usually at its most handsome in late summer.

However, if you'd like to spice up the flowerbed, try sweet potato. This is another newcomer to bedding plants available in Sweden, and it comes with lime green, copper brown, or dark, almost black-red, foliage. Leafy plants such as coleus and beefsteak plant are well known; they're look-alikes and both need damp soil to grow their best. They thrive in a well-tended flowerbed and come in many color combinations.

Grass plants have decorative leaves, and in late summer they also sport attractive flower plumes and panicles. Annual grasses are also recent additions to our selection of bedding plants, and combining them with roses can add a real edge to the flowerbed. It's not a good choice for a romantic garden, but it can look very smart in a contemporary setting that includes lots of stone elements in the landscape. Love grass and foxtail barley are like gossamer and shining, while grey hair grass is more punk, and pearl millet is incredibly showy with its purple-red foliage. There is currently a lot of interest in ornamental grasses, and thrilling new varieties can be sought out at garden centers.

Summer flowers you can sow yourself

Many of the most beautiful flowers are not available as plants, because they're directly sown in the flowerbed. Many of them make fantastic companion plants for roses, but don't expect good results if you sow the seeds directly under the roses in the bed, as the seeds will have a hard time competing with the roses' roots. You'll have more success if you plant small plants between the roses instead.

Starter plants are easy to cultivate if you give them a bit of help at the beginning. Follow the instructions on the seed packet—sow the seeds far apart, in shallow boxes filled with planting soil. Water them and leave them to grow at room temperature. When they've germinated, move them to a greenhouse, balcony, deck, or patio; the seedlings need light and protection from wind and weather. Let the seedlings grow for a few weeks, and water and fertilize them during this time with a weak solution. Set the young plants in carefully loosened soil around the roses, and water. Make sure to irrigate the plants at least once a week during the first few weeks after transplanting out so they develop.

You can try all kinds of flowers—from marigolds to cornflower and corn marigold. Here are some suggestions for plants that come in many varieties. Choose your flowers by color and height specifications on the back of the seed packet.

Atlasflower, also known as godetia or farewell-to-spring, is an old-fashioned summer flower that's easy to grow. It's a perfect candidate for a romantic flowerbed with delicate flowers in pink, lilac, and white. The plants can be placed pretty close together and they flower over a long stretch of time. California poppy is similar to the atlasflower but comes in other colors. Bright yellow and orange, fire red, and creamy yellow are colors for them. The flower is simple and shimmers like silk.

Peony poppies come in absolutely magnificent colors and should not be excluded from the garden. They thread their high, slender stalks up past the roses to offer a short but glorious flower display. Love-in-a-mist looks ravishing among the roses; its fennel-like foliage is excellent filler, and many new lovely varieties in blue or white are available now. They're highly decorative even when their blooms are spent, thanks to their elegant seed capsules.

Annual delphinium doesn't germinate reliably, so it needs to be pre-cultivated in a box to ensure a positive outcome. There are many beautiful varieties with delicate spires in hues of white, blue, lilac, and pink. Its purple variety is especially attractive when combined with white and yellow roses. The annual larkspur (which differs slightly from delphiniums), and rocket larkspur are both particularly suited to roses, and add that special cottage garden charm to flowerbeds.

The spider plant grows tall and lanky, with dainty flowers that flutter above or between the roses. The plant comes in short- or long-stemmed varieties, and its flowers enchant in pink, violet, and white. They reach at least 50 cm (1½') in height; occasionally you can see some varieties available as plants. Cosmos—or Mexican aster, as it's also called—is a slightly sturdier plant than the spider plant. This is another great filler, with its white and pinkish violet flowers and ferny foliage. Its height varies from 40 cm to 1 m (1¾' to 3¼'). It too can sometimes be purchased as a young plant.

Nasturtium is a vigorous and brightly colored summer flower. The climbing variety will easily strangle a rose plant, so in order to accommodate bedding roses, it's best to go with a bushy or less aggressive, trailing variety of nasturtium. It is easy to put attractively vibrant color combinations together with this flower, which is incredibly easy to grow, a great filler, and will cover the ground completely.

Livingstone daisy is a succulent with silk shimmering flowers in brilliant colors. It's drought resistant and has a spreading growth habit. It makes a shining mat of flowers in, among other colors, yellow, orange, and salmon. It's a bit of an odd companion for a rose, but it is lovely nonetheless.

The atlas flower is just one of the old-fashioned flowers made for the rose bed. It is rare to find this plant, but it is easily sown in the home garden. Although this picture was taken in October, the flower is still in bloom.

Mexican asters are lanky flowers that are supported by the roses, while their fennel-like leaves are fillers between the rose plants.

Fall beauty in a surprising combination of maiden grass and roses.

Yellow coneflowers and roses are a traditional combination suggested by vintage books on roses. The salmon rose 'Feuerwerk' is quite hardy and has survived in Swedish zone 4 and in stiff clay soil, both difficult settings that kill many other roses in winter.

Roses in the fall

Many modern roses continue to flower into the fall as if there were no such thing as winter. They might eventually start to look a bit tired, but in good company the rose bed can still look nice for quite a while. Perennials do help, of course, but you can also add purchased, ornamental bedding plants. Many plants, whether they're summer flowers, herbs, or perennials, are forced into bloom in the fall. They're considered annuals, but several of them can survive winter. They might be unreliably hardy depending on where they're planted in the country, but they still make fine bedding plants since they can tolerate a bit of a chill. Elegant ornamental grasses can also give the flowerbed a much-needed late season shot of color, even if they don't have any flowers. It's well worth your time to give some extra thought and care to the flowerbed in the fall. Those last flowers are greatly loved, much the same way as the very first, brightly colored flowers of spring.

Perennials and late summer flowering

There aren't many perennials that return year after year that also bloom in the fall. Their natural growth cycle dictates that flowering is over in summer to set seed for fall, hence the few remaining late perennial bloomers out there.

Chinese anemone, also known as Japanese anemone, bears elegant pink or white flowers high up on delicate but wiry stalks. Its foliage protects the bare rose canes and trunks. Anemones can become invasive if they adapt well to the location—in fact they carry the 'invasive plant' warning in the south of Sweden—although they have difficulty surviving in damp ground. Hybrid anemone, hardy grape leaf anemone and Japanese anemone are all different varieties of the same flower, but they're not all that different from one another.

Autumn phlox won't be affected by powdery mildew if it gets plenty of water. This is an excellent companion to the red stripy rose 'Candy Cover'. Tree mallows can be seen in the background.

Fall blooming companion plants in the rose bed

Chinese or **Japanese anemone**, *Anemone hupehensis*; pale pink and white flowers.

Aster, *Aster*, there many kinds with different flowering times.

Clematis, non-climbing, *Clematis heracleifolia*; elegant, blue trumpet-shaped blooms from August on; its hardiness is uncertain.

Solitary clematis, *Clematis integrifolia*, flowers from July onwards, in blue or pink.

Ground clematis, *Clematis recta*, many small white flowers on a robust semi-high clematis that needs support, as it can grow up to 150 cm (5').

Purple coneflower, *Echinacea purpurea*, wonderful upright flower, pinkish red petals.

Globe thistle, *Echinops*; a most impressive silver blue thistle.

Sea holly, *Eryngium*, silvery green grey or violet blue and thistle-like.

Fall phlox, *Phlox paniculata*, many varieties, lots of colors, but drought intolerant so it needs regular watering.

Rudbeckia, *Rudbeckia*, brightly yellow fall classic, a reliable flowerbed staple.

Giant goldenrod, *Solidago gigantea*, somewhat invasive, but very handsome when contained.

Fall phlox is a late summer bloomer that lasts long into the fall. It needs damp soil to avoid getting powdery mildew, even if some types are considered mildew resistant. They make a good companion plant for roses if the bed is irrigated regularly. Phlox is a great plant, as it comes in many colors and heights, and can flower either early or late in the season. Many varieties are scented; they're very lovely in a vase with some late bloom roses. The tallest and most robust types of phlox are best planted together with shrub roses.

New York aster, like fall phlox, needs damp, nutrient-rich soil. If you can provide this, it will display flowers in many pink, red, and violet hues. Select color and variety carefully, as its flowers are quite similar in height but flowering times can vary widely. Some late-bloomers never have the time to open fully in the north of Sweden, while others will grow into very tall, sturdy clusters that are far too big to fit in a flowerbed. They're most suited as partners to burnet roses and other shrub roses. The smaller asters sold for containers and window boxes can also be used as bedding plants in the rose bed. These are perennials, but in years following planting they won't come in as low, and they'll flower later than in the first year.

Exceptionally elegant

There are also more unusual plants with drawn-out flowering that may last well into the fall. Even if they don't show the same profusion of flowers, they make up for it by blooming for a very long time. Among them are some exceptionally elegant rose companion plants.

Solitary clematis and non-climbing clematis are perennial clematis that won't climb. Typically the flowers are blue bells and nod, but there are several other varieties. They have weak stems and fit well among roses, which provide them with support; these elegant plants really come into their own amongst the roses. They bloom in summer, from June to September or later, depending on their type. Even if they're somewhat uncertain in hardiness further up in Sweden, they can still put forth an unusually glorious late summer flowering. Ground clematis is hardier and produces lots of small white flowers, and is also a good companion plant to robust bedding roses.

Globe thistle is a stiff and tall plant with silvery blue spikes growing on top of a rounded head. It flowers in July and August, but is lovely even when the individual flowers have wilted. If unchecked, the globe thistle can spread pretty quickly, but is perfect as a kind of exclamation point among old-fashioned shrub roses or a modern white bedding rose. Sea holly is very similar to the globe thistle in coloring—it's also silver blue and thistle-like—but it differs in that it has several small burs on its branched stems. The Alpine sea holly is its hardier cousin, and can even become invasive. Flat sea holly is found in varieties that are silver, tinged with blue.

Red coneflower is a perennial that has quickly become extremely popular in Sweden. It's wonderful in a rose bed, where it's a veritable butterfly magnet. The large brown center button protrudes like on all rudbeckias, and the petals are intensely pink. Many new varieties are being introduced in orange-yellow shades; even white versions exist now. It's a sturdy and rewarding plant with a long bloom period, and is beautiful even when it has

Stonecrop has attractive foliage during most of the summer, but doesn't flower until fall. The light green leaves are beautiful against the roses' dark leaves. Stonecrop 'Stardust' should have white flowers, but it will occasionally sport a few single pink flowers, too.

wilted. Hardiness is uncertain in cold climates and it needs well-drained soil. The pink coneflower is the hardiest of the lot.

Bold colors

Rudbeckia—of which brown-eyed Susan is a well-known variety—has yellow flowers with a dark brown center button. This is an older perennial often recommended as a companion plant for red roses in older gardening books. Red and bright yellow is a strong color combination, very much in favor years ago. If you choose pale yellow roses instead of red, however, the flowerbed will be more harmonious in color. Rudbeckia is both rewarding and easy to cultivate, and its growth habit is sturdy and upright. Giant goldenrod is a more daring choice of plants to set among roses, according to a famous and experienced rose grower. Goldenrod produces small, bright yellow flowers that attract beneficial insects, and flowers over a long period. It's a vigorous grower, so pick varieties that are low growing and smaller to be on the safe side.

More risky, yet still elegant, is to plant different varieties of loosestrife as companions to roses. Some caution is advised, especially with the tall yellow loosestrife, which can easily take over. It's a familiar but beautiful plant, easy to grow, but it definitely needs a firm hand. Its relative, moneywort, can also become a problem; it's regularly used as an edging plant, both in borders and in containers, but it has creeping runners that take root wherever they can get a foothold, thus behaving like weeds. All the same, it's such a good groundcover, with its beautiful light green leaves and bright yellow flowers. Radiant color also can be found in the yellow-leafed variation of moneywort, which doesn't have such an aggressive growth habit.

Attractive plants with contrasting foliage

There may be fewer flowers in the fall, but plants with unusual and striking leaves can still brighten the rose bed. The well-known stonecrop stays handsome over a prolonged period; its large, sturdy foliage acts as filler as early as June. However, it can also grow a bit too large and crowd out the roses. New, smaller varieties in contrasting colors are thus recommended; sun and dry soil is their preferred medium. Roses paired with heuchera look striking, which grows happily as companion plant, as long as the rose bed is irrigated regularly. You can create

At times, when the soil and location are just right, you can succeed putting together seemingly impossible combinations. Ostrich fern and hosta (also known as plantain lily) favor part-shade light and really damp soil, yet still manage to make delightful companion plants for roses.

tremendous color combinations with under plantings of heuchera. The last few years have seen the introduction of many delicate leaf colors, ranging from caramel to apricot, and almost black red over to silver and green. The leaves cover the ground and grow like pillows, sprouting delicate flowers that usually appear in early summer but that stick around for quite a while. Lime green leaves under yellow and orange roses; dark red leaves beneath white and pale pink roses; brandy brown with roses striped pink, red, and white reminiscent of candy canes—give your imagination free reign. These plants' flowers are most commonly white, cream-colored, or pale pink, but more intense red varieties exist, too. While many heucheras are sold as bedding plants in the fall, it's perhaps a bit much to ask of them to survive winter; they do however impart a new fresh look to the rose bed. Contrasting leaf colors can also be found in bedding plants such as sage, lavender cotton, curry plant, and stonecrop. Other, early flowering perennials can be bought as fall flowering plants. Growers prune them in spring to hold back their flowering, so these can add extra fall colors to the flowerbed. Fall flowers can be mixed in with ornamental grasses (either summer plantings or new transplants), with their wispy flower heads and handsome leaves.

Low-growing bushes between roses give the flowerbed shape year round. Potentilla—otherwise known as cinquefoil—and Russian sage flower in late summer. They need to be pruned hard each spring so they don't grow too large and hide the roses.

Long-lasting companion plants

Low, round-shaped bushes are fine-looking elements in the rose bed. They're somewhat sturdy in growth and fill in well between tall flower stalks and sprawling rose canes. They stay strong even in the rain, when roses and flowers can start to look defeated. Bushes are excellent for pepping up flowerbeds, especially in early spring and late fall, on condition that they grow really low and don't take over the bed. Pick bushes that can stand a hard pruning, but that also provide nice color and shape. It's merely a bonus if they flower, as many bushes grow handsomely colored leaves. Beautiful foliage lasts the entire summer, in contrast to flowers that can sometimes wilt in as little as a week.

Steady companions

Many bushes come in large and small varieties. Potentilla or spirea can grow to 40 cm or 140 cm (1¼' to 4½') tall. Keep in mind that just because you buy a small bush doesn't mean it's going to stay small. Do some research to find out how tall the bush will be in 10 years' time, and select varieties that won't exceed 1 m (3.25') in height. Some bushes are still okay even if they grow taller because they can be pruned down to size; however, not all bushes react well to a lot of pruning. There isn't much diversity in bushes suited to be companion plants to roses, but those that work come in different varieties. The bushes can be a good bit taller if they're going to be the backdrop of the flowerbed, or used as an adjoining hedge.

Barberries are very resilient and cushion-shaped with yellow, lime green, variegated, or red leaves. They need trimming each year to keep their attractive shape. They green up early and last long into the fall.

Boxwood and roses make a well-loved combination. Boxwood is often grown as a hedge around the rose bed and its glossy green leaves bring out the roses in all their glory. There are big differences between the different types of boxwood, however, even though they all look the same. Choose a low growing boxwood, otherwise it'll grow past the roses and cover them. In colder climates try more hardy and slow-growing varieties such as 'Polar' and 'Green Mountain', or the faster growing 'Green Velvet'.

Potentilla is fabulous; it's long blooming and comes in many different shades.

Bushes with colored foliage can bring out the color of the roses. Low-growing barberries with yellow or red leaves make perfect companion plantings.

Potentilla (cinquefoil)

Below are low growing and compact varieties that are well suited to flowerbeds. Some varieties might need to be special ordered.

'Daydawn' has a slightly sprawling growth habit, yellow shimmery leaves and mild apricot-colored flowers.

'Estleigh Cream'; bears creamy white flowers and beautiful grey-green leaves.

'Godstar' is a typical bright yellow variety.

'Hopleys Orange', bears orange flowers.

'Kobold' has yellow flowers on a wide, low-growing wide bush.

'Limelight' flowers are soft lime yellow, and its foliage consists of fine palm-like leaves.

'Mango Tango' is a new variety with two-toned red and yellow flowers that lighten to orange in warm weather.

'Pink Beauty'/**'Lovely Pink'** features very pink, almost cherry-colored flowers on a compact plant.

'Pink Queen' bears light pink flowers that can shift to white in warm summers.

'Red Robin' is a red variety that is an improvement on earlier red varieties, but is still a bit more orange red than true red.

Japanese spireas are low, late summer blooming bushes with pink or white flowers. They can be pruned all the way to the ground each spring, and grow into a 30 cm to 70 cm (1' to 2¼') pillowy mound. They are green very early, around the same time tulips are in flower, and bring color and shape in early spring. Varieties that have different colored leaves are at their most intense in spring when they leaf out. The following are very beautiful specimens: 'Firelight' with young, orange leaves and dark pink flowers; 'Goldmound' has light yellow-green leaves and pink flowers; 'Shirobana', a green-leafed plant bears both red and white flowers. There are also several varieties that feature bright green leaves and bloom in reddish pink or white. If you prune them hard you'll enjoy their foliage first, and then in late summer the flowers fill in among the roses. Choose carefully so you get compatible colors.

Exuberant flowering

Potentilla blooms over a long period and, along with the rose, is the summer's longest-flowering plant. The flowers look like buttercups in red, pink, yellow, orange, and white. Lime green flowers with white roses and purple butterfly bush look gorgeous; pink potentilla with pink roses, white pearly everlasting and blue Russian sage can be very pretty too. Bright yellow potentilla together with pale yellow roses makes a striking pair, as do orange varieties with orange or red roses. Long flowering, low growing white potentilla with its grey-green leaves, matched with the pink 'The Fairy' rose, looks absolutely stunning on a sunny slope. Prune the potentilla each year at the same time as the roses so it keeps its nice round shape. Pruning delays the flowering a bit, but it's needed anyway to keep the bush low.

Larger roses can be planted with more robust bushes. This picture illustrates an unusual combination of roses and tamarisk, a plant hardy only in the south of Sweden. It's an extravagant flower display in a companion planting with mock orange and oxeye daisies. Keep in mind that this is on the island of Hven, which is in Swedish climate zone 1. In colder climates the tamarisk won't grow anywhere near as big.

Low bushes form the frame of the rose bed

Japanese barberry, *Berberis thunbergii* has several low-growing varieties with red or yellow foliage. Swedish zones 3–4.

Butterfly bush, *Buddleja davidii*, sun and drought resistant, large bush that can be pruned hard. Swedish zone 3.

Boxwood, *Buxus*, choose low-growing varieties, preferably; 'Polar' is hardy in Swedish zone 5.

Bluebeard, *Caryopteris*, blue, late summer bloom; Swedish zone 1.

Wild or **California lilacs**, *Ceanothus*, early summer bloom in lavender lilac; Swedish zone 1.

Chiliotrichum, *Chiliotrichum diffusum*, Swedish zone 1–2.

Potentilla or **shrubby cinquefoil**, *Potentilla fruticosa*, many colors, Swedish zone 4–7, depending on variety.

Japanese spirea, *Spiraea japonica*, varieties sporting yellowish leaves, summer flowers in pink or white. Swedish zones 3–4.

Weigela, *Weigela*, there are several new varieties with colored leaves and flowers in pinkish red tones. Swedish zones 1–2.

Delicate flowering bushes

There are several more bushes that flower simultaneously with the roses; many smaller varieties of uncertain hardiness can be tried out in the rose bed. Typically they shouldn't be planted on their own, but in a protected bed in a sunny spot, they might just make it. The following bushes are delicate plants for Swedish zones 1–3:

Butterfly bush is a large and robust bush, especially in the south of Sweden. Further north it often freezes. This is not too bad a thing in a flowerbed, where it can grow anew from the ground each spring or not get too large.

Weigela comes in both large and small bushes. The flowers that arrive in early summer are funnel-shaped, and usually pink or red. New, lower-growing, more exotic varieties combine flowers with ornamental foliage and are suitable in size; they grow between 50 cm and 1 m (1⅗' to 3¼') tall, but they're so new that we don't quite know how they'll perform in the long run. Interesting specimens to try are 'Brigela' with its yellow-green variegated foliage and red flowers; 'Monet' with white rose-patterned leaves and pink flowers; 'Cappucino' with green leaves and pink flowers that have a hint of mocha in them; 'Minor Black' with dark brown-red leaves and reddish pink flowers. 'Minuet' is more familiar to us, with flowers in pink to red, and foliage that develops handsome fall colors. They're usually hardy in Swedish zone 2–3. When included in a

flowerbed, it may not be too critical that parts of their branches freeze, since they re-grow from the ground each spring. There will be fewer flowers, but the foliage on young branches with new shoots is always lovely.

Bluebeard is only hardy in the southernmost part Sweden. It flowers late in the season with blue lilac flowers, and features spicy and aromatic silver green leaves. It often suffers from winter damage but can somehow flower anyway. It goes exceptionally well with roses, Russian sage, and potentilla. 'Heavenly Blue' will grow to around 1 m (1¼').

Wild lilac (California lilac) blooms in early summer with blue flowers. It's hardy but just barely so, in Skåne, in the south of Sweden. If its branches are frost damaged it will not produce any flowers, since it only blooms on the past year's growth. So you're taking a chance by planting it, even if you have a sunny spot for it in a rose bed in Swedish zone 1.

Chiliotrichum, also called bush marguerite, is a dainty bush with daisy-like flowers. The foliage has lance-shaped mild grey-green leaves, and the bush is low with a slightly sprawling growth habit. It's hardy in Swedish zone 2, but even this plant should have a try-out in the rose bed; its visual effect is that of large daisies planted among the roses. Although it isn't an overwhelming bloomer, chiliotrichum is a sturdy grower and it flowers a long time.

Ideas for using roses

A rose garden needn't be spacious. The entryway to a condo—here, an area roughly 2 x 2 m (65' x 65') in size—can be turned into a flowering oasis. Roses that climb, a border of bedding roses with summer annuals and yellow star-of-Bethlehem as companion plants, produce long-lasting, abundant blooms.

There are many approaches to designing and setting up your own garden of roses. Thanks to the fact that they flower so abundantly and over such a long period of time, you don't need to plant a lot of roses to turn the space into a flowering oasis. A climbing rose, two or three modern shrub roses, a few low-growing groundcover roses, and five to seven perennials make up a tidy collection that can be planted into an array of different combinations. This is rose cultivation that requires neither a lot of space nor a lot of work, and is possible to set up even in the small garden patch of a condo.

Anyone can create a rose garden. There's no need for a large area; 2 x 2 m (65' x 65') is enough for many roses. In order to plant a lot of roses in a small space, pick both low-growing and tall roses, which then can be combined with a climbing rose. Start by choosing the climber, as there's a larger assortment to choose from among the other types. It's always easier to find bedding roses to suit a climber than vice versa. The climber should be hardy and flower over a long stretch of time; it also needs to be healthy and have beautiful blooms that look good against other decorative elements, such as a trellis and window frames. Once the climbing rose has been selected, add companion plants in form of different roses in matching or contrasting colors, and other plants that will prolong the flowering period.

Traditional or custom variations

You can combine roses in multiple ways, but be mindful of the plants' characteristics and colors. Pink and white is always charming, especially when paired with blue. Red and white is traditional and can be very striking against a green or white house exterior, but less so against a deep Falu (the traditional old Swedish cottage color) red. Yellow and orange looks smart against a 1970s house built out of dark brick, but would be a total mismatch with a red cottage. Traditional edging plants are blue lavender and blue garden catnip; blue plants look attractive with all kinds of roses. But picking a different rose can turn a combination into something much more unique, which can then be customized to your house, walkway, or overall entrance.

Old-fashioned rose gardens

In monasteries, roses were grown in the herb garden for use as medicinal plants. Oldest is the apothecary's rose and the stripy mundy (*Rosa mundi*) rose, which were regularly planted in the middle of a quadrant and then surrounded by low-growing lavender hedges; thus, lavenders and roses are known as a traditional horticultural pairing. Medicinal plants and roses have had a long relationship throughout history, so today's herb gardens would be remiss not to have roses planted in them. For an old-world touch, plant herbs in the rose bed, too.

Many herbs need warmth and a slightly dry environment, but their most essential requirement is sunshine. Sage, thyme, southern wormwood, and hyssop are excellent planted by roses, as is lavender. Both wormwood and hyssop have growth habits similar to lavender, but both are hardier than lavender and can be used as hedges in herb gardens further north in Sweden.

A quadrant...

The layout is of utmost importance when you mimic an old-fashioned rose garden; it combines herbs and roses in a quadrant surrounded by a low hedge. The hedge is chosen to suit the climate; in the middle of the quadrant you'll plant a tree rose, which can be planted directly in the ground or left in a decorative pot. In cold climates, the tree rose is moved inside in winter.

In the quadrant's corners you'll plant roses, your pick of one type or different varieties. The ground of the quadrant between the roses is planted with thyme, or herbs you use more frequently that thrive in sun and drier soil. Both parsley and chives are lovely edging plants, as long as they have enough moisture. One option for imitating the quadrants of yore is to cover the ground with crushed brick or mussel shells.

...or a few

A rose garden can also consist of four small quadrants and a central area. Place a tree rose or a shrub rose at the

A modern-day rose garden in a paved area.

A traditional rose garden surrounded by a boxwood hedge.

A rose garden in an allotment; it doesn't really matter that it's a bit bare in the spring, because it's not a period of time when the gardener is constantly on site.

The same rose garden, this time in summer. July and August, when the allotment garden is at its most beautiful, coincides with the time when it's most used and enjoyed.

center. In the quadrants, which can be as small as 40 cm x 40 cm (1.3' x 1.3') each, plant a rose or some herbs—sage or mint, for instance. (To prevent the mint from spreading too far, place it in a small bottomless pail dug down into the ground.) Quadrants are a traditional plan that can be repeated with the same or different plants. Plant a combination of flowers and herbs in a pattern by placing roses in two diagonal quadrants, and sturdy herb plants in each of the other two. Make the quadrants 40 cm x 40 cm (1.3' x 1.3') or larger. Use the same kinds of plants, or different ones, for the hedges: boxwood, lavender, hyssop, or wormwood; even beautiful stones make lovely edging. You can even create a chessboard with roses in many small squares and stones to demarcate them. It's easy to care for and breathtaking, but the roses must be watered regularly as the quadrants dry out quickly. The small entrance to a condo can thus become a flowering nook with plenty of glorious color, instead of a dull patch of dry grass pleasing to no one.

Beautiful rose combinations

Delightful colors

The white climber 'White Nights' is new and interesting, and is a lovely backdrop to the light pink shrub rose 'Claire Renaissance'. Combined with white baby's breath, light pink garden thyme, and, in contrast, a blood red maiden pink 'Samos', it makes for a delicate yet vibrantly colorful mix. White is a popular color in Sweden, and white handsomely combines with other whites. The bedding rose 'Lion's-Rose' in creamy white with a hint of pink, in front of a white climbing rose, in tandem with the low-growing 'White Cover' and cut-leaf daisy in lavender blue, is breathtaking. If you prefer a totally white setting, let lamb's ears cover the ground and the white catchfly peek up and out between the low-growing roses, instead of the cut-leaf daisy.

For a real cutting-edge touch, let a white climbing rose and the groundcover rose 'Swany' pair up with the scented 'Black & White Minstrels'—a dianthus in white and as near to black as it's possible to get. That combo will certainly be a real eye-catcher! Add an extra accent with ornamental grass pearl millet 'Purple Majesty', with its tall, slim cylindrical flower heads in reddish brown. Buy the ornamental grass as a plant and place it in a large container between the roses for maximum effect. The container will be hidden between the roses, leaving the grass to draw the eye to the staging.

Lemon tones

Dark walls and red bricks are commonplace, and they pair well with yellow. Yellow climber 'Leverkusen', together with white shrub or bedding roses, gives off a cool lemon vibe that can be beautifully paired with the white petals and yellow buttons of oxeye daisies. These can be combined with potentilla 'Limelight', which is pruned hard each spring; or, mild blue-violet cranesbill, windflower, garden catnip, lesser calamint 'Blue Cloud', gentian sage 'Cambridge Blue' and verbena 'Polaris' in icy lilac (these are bedding plants; the rest of the plants are hardy).

Yellow and lilac are contrasting colors that are always striking when seen together. If you want to add even more color to the mix, choose a climbing rose in bright yellow, such as 'Golden Gate' or 'Goldener Olymp'. A spring bloom can be purple mini pansies, followed by woodland sage 'Caradonna' and ornamental oregano 'Herrenhausen'. If you're looking for utmost exquisiteness, plant late-blooming pale blue-violet clematis near the rose. Lavender, planted alongside with the woodland sage, will further prolong the flowering period.

An old fashioned entrance, where the pelargoniums match the roses.

Red roses are lovely against the backdrop of white houses, and help create a welcoming entrance.

Warming yellow orange

The old climbing rose 'Alchemyst' is creamy yellow with a shift to apricot pink. It's very elegant, but the flowering period is, alas, quite short. The new 'Kordes' seems to have that same color and is allegedly longer blooming. Choose a shrub rose to go with them, such as 'Westerland', which shifts from orange to pink, depending on the weather. Beautiful, and in the same color palette, is the cottage rose 'Linnaeus', with its mass of single bronze-yellow flowers, and likewise, the smaller 'Flaming Cover'. Add bedding plants in white or silver grey, like the curry plant. Lamb's ears are silver-grey perennials that form a muted mat beneath the roses. For extra shot of rich color, add some orange and red, but pick your shade carefully; Maltese (Jerusalem) cross, and yarrow 'Terracotta' and 'Walter Funke' are good selections. They're strong and bright orange red.

If it's more of a pure yellow color you're after, choose the 'Sophia Renaissance' bedding rose instead, together with 'Olympic Palace' as low-growing groundcover. My own yellow combination begins with forsythia and cushion spurge, followed by yellow roses—tall and low-growing—as well as yellow lilies. In late summer, an Indian aster flowers in variegated yellowy green, which works well with the lime green accent of the cushion spurge. The aster is mostly included in the flowerbed because of its foliage color. Its flower is pale lilac with a yellow eye, providing mild shades of contrasting color.

Romantic pink

Pink can easily be combined with many colors. White, blue, purple, other shades of pink, and red are all incredibly rewarding. If you choose colors that change subtly, you can match the color of a flower's eye with another flower's petals or foliage in that particular shade. Pink can have a hint of yellow in it, or sometimes salmon or cold pink going on mauve. You can bring these undertones to the forefront by mixing them with other plants that reinforce those tints. A yellow-apricot climbing rose like 'Alchemyst', for instance, has a touch of pink in it, which makes it get on very well with a salmon-pink rose like 'Läckö'. The groundcover 'Flower Carpet' is without a doubt an icy pink rose—almost lilac—so it's a great match

A profusion of glorious rose blooms is the result of a combination of climbing roses, bedding roses and low-growing groundcover roses below them. You can choose roses in either a single color or in many different shades—just follow your personal taste. Here is pink 'Aloha' with yellow 'Alchemyst'; they're both lovely, but sadly they don't bloom continuously; these beauties only last a few short weeks.

for the baby pink climber 'Rosenholm'. All pink shades look gorgeous in tandem with classic blue edging plants like wood sage, lavender, and garden catnip.

White and the climber 'Rosenholm', or one of the new climbing Max roses from Kordes, such as the dark pink 'Laguna' or the pale lilac-tinted 'Jasmina'—make an exquisitely delicate combination. Pearly everlasting, lamb's ears, sneezewort, baby's breath are all good whites, as is modern garden pink in white and pink shades.

The pale porcelain pink 'New Dawn', or the fuller form of the same rose called 'Awakening', is recommended for colder climates. It flowers with abandon for a few weeks and then it repeats a little less, but long into fall. This is a vigorous and robust grower than can be heartily recommended for an archway, a porch, or a pergola. The light pink color goes very well with low growing 'Sommerwind' or the slightly darker pink 'Lovely Fairy'. This is a hardy and reliable combination. Pearly everlasting's white flowers will light up below the roses; they provide color long into fall, after 'New Dawn' has finished its season.

Red, the ultimate rose

Red roses are what dreams are made of. Red is a strong color, and gorgeous against a white, grey, blue, or pink house exterior. Thanks to all its green leaves it looks good even against a Falu red house, but it truly comes into its own against a lighter backdrop. Blazing red is popular among climbing roses. Of summer's repeat bloomers, 'Sympathie' is the most familiar. 'Amadeus' is newer, but it only grows to a height of 2 m (6.5'). The well-known 'Flammentanz' is an absolute favorite in colder climates.

You can mix red roses with plants of just about any other color. A classic combination is blue and white with a true red. Tall, blue delphiniums or larkspurs, along with oxeye daisies and a low-growing bedding rose like 'H. C. Andersen' is the essence of elegance. The low-growing 'White Cover', groundcover 'Diamant', or chalk-white 'Swany' are all superb combined with a red climbing rose. The dark red shrub rose 'Nadia Renaissance' is well worth trying with red climber and white groundcover varieties. A red groundcover rose looks stunning together with a red climber. The single 'Golden Eye', accented by its clearly visible yellow center, looks good with both red and yellow flowers. Yellow perennials like rudbeckia, coreopsis, and European goldenrod will enjoy the company of 'Flammentanz' and 'Golden Eye' in colder areas.

A more unusual combination that can produce a strong visual impact is a red climbing rose with both red and dark red roses—the sisters 'Maria' and 'Nadia Renaissance' come to mind, or the full 'Leonardo da Vinci' with the single 'Romanze' along with the small flowers of 'The Red Fairy'.

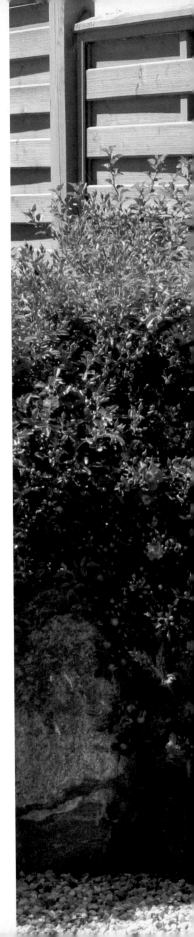

'Tommelise' is a rose with a spreading growth habit. Here it covers the whole pot. Because it's planted in a container, it can be placed on a dry and hard driveway.

POTTED ROSES

Roses can be grown in containers in many different ways, and several roses have been developed especially for this purpose. They can be combined with other plants or other roses, and can adapt to a wide range of environments. Tree roses grown in pots can provide height, and climbing roses in planters can be used as a privacy screen. A drab spot in the garden, a bare balcony or deck, or a hard-surfaced patio can all be freshened up with help of container-grown roses. Roses can also be grown in containers if they lack hardiness, as the pot can be placed in a more protected area during the coldest part of the year.

Roses as bedding plants and houseplants

Roses are vibrant plants in pots and planters. The same companies that breed garden roses, namely Kordes, Meilland and Poulsen, also deal in potted roses; all sell varieties on the Swedish market. These are special miniature roses with small leaves and diminutive flowers. Varieties are propagated through cuttings that are put straight into pots, then topped, and then left to develop, grow and flower. They're grown in greenhouses, and require a lot of light to produce beautiful flowers.

Potted roses can also be used as bedding plants in smaller pots and window boxes. They flower through the summer, but make sure to treat them as an annual. If planted out in the flowerbed, they will stay quite small and will have difficulty coping in winter. They overwinter better in a really cold climate with a proper snow cover, than in Skåne, Sweden's southern-most province, with its unpredictable winter weather. Take extra care when placing them outside, as the leaves scorch easily in the sun; give them time to acclimatize to the strong sunlight.

'Crystal Palace' is part of a group sold as Palace roses, which are good for growing in containers. Flowers and leaves are standard sized, while the plant itself is small.

Different colors and varieties

Potted roses are seldom sold with a nametag, which is a pity because they all have a name, and the roses differ from one another. The smallest varieties will only reach about 20 cm (7.8") high and they have approximately 2 cm (less than 1"), perfect, miniature, hybrid tea rose-like blooms. The larger, slightly sturdier varieties are typically sold in larger pots and can reach a height of approximately 40 cm (1.30'). The flowers are also larger, still beautifully hybrid tea shaped but with slightly thicker stems. All potted roses should be placed in direct light and sunshine, but they should not be left to dry out. Water them regularly—about once a day—with a weak fertilizer solution. Cut off flowers as they wither to encourage new buds to emerge quicker.

By all means, plant container roses with companion summer flowers that also enjoy direct sun. Cascading lobelia, verbena, and twinspur are delightful when planted together with miniature roses. Heliotrope and purple pansies add a romantic touch; daisies make them very pretty. Feather celosia (cockscomb) and ornamental grasses produce boldly colored combinations. Do not hold back. Give your imagination free reign!

Specific varieties suited for containers

There are many ways to grow regular-sized roses in containers, if you wish. You can pick a rose that you plan to keep only over the summer. You can choose anything that takes your fancy in color and shape, as long as the planter is large enough to accommodate it. If you opt for a variety of rose that is hardy, you can always plant it in the ground once summer is over. If you want to keep the rose in a pot over several years, you'll have to take the size of the rose into account; for a container rose to make it over a long period of time, it needs to be a smaller specimen. Roses with small leaves and flowers are called miniature roses, but there's a significant difference between small roses sold as potted plants and large container 'miniature roses.' Smaller roses adapted to growing in containers are also sold in product groups or in series. One popular series, from Denmark, is called 'Patio Hit'; those roses are rarely sold in Sweden, however, because they're less hardy than bedding roses. The series named Palace roses is more common; they're low-growing roses with full-sized

Container planted roses and summer flowers in a brick-tiled yard.

The rose 'Perennial Blush' is sold as a flowering potted plant to be used as summer flower. In the background is clematis 'Tartu'.

flowers and foliage. They're used both as small bedding roses and as container roses, and come in several varieties. They reach a height of 40 cm to 60 cm (1.30' to 1.90') and all varieties bear two names, the first one being unique to the plant, followed by the series name 'Palace'. Low-growing bedding roses, like the spreading cover roses (see 'Groundcover roses,' p. 44), have diminutive flowers and small leaves, and are eminently suitable to grow in containers. They also grow to a height of around 40 cm to 60 cm (1.30' to 1.90'). Groundcover roses make beautiful container plants, with their canes spilling over the side. Even slightly larger groundcover roses like 'The Fairy' can look handsome in a larger planter or box; the trailing canes will end up hiding the planter or box entirely.

Deliciously lime-green potted rose in the company of yellow moneywort.

Standard roses require large containers

Most standard sized roses can be grown in containers as long as the planter or pot is roomy. Sturdy planters with trellises full of climbing roses make gorgeous wind barriers and privacy shields. Shrub roses can become tall, but they also grow wide, which makes them less suited to being planted in containers. Climbing roses can be trained against a support, and you can trim their width; shrub roses simply take up too much space. Roses grown in containers that can't be moved need to be hardy in order to survive winter. Less hardy container roses should be relocated to a protected area, or they need to be adequately covered, in order to cope with colder temperatures.

Care for container roses

You can buy flowering bedding roses in containers in the summer. Both climbers and bedding roses need to be potted up immediately, and they need larger containers because roses are seldom sold in pots that are large enough for them. The rose will grow much better after being potted up; the container should hold at least 20 to 30 liters (5.25 to 8 gallons) of soil. Large pots and planters quickly become heavy, so use plastic or fiber clay planters if you want to be able to move them.

Container roses come with relatively small amounts of soil to grow in. The more soil it has, the bigger its capacity for storing nutrients and water; nevertheless, it will never match being planted directly into the ground. It's not very efficient to add in nutrients through the soil's surface; roses benefit more from having liquid fertilizer added to the irrigation can, and receiving some nutrients at each watering. The Swedish product called Blomstra, or other complete fertilizer (follow manufacturer's recommendation), can be administered in increments of 1 ml (0.03 fl oz) per quart of water, and will work for all summer flowers and flowering garden plants.

Drainage holes

Container roses are even more dependent on regular irrigation than roses that are planted in the ground. Potted roses can't be allowed to dry out completely, because they'll droop and won't bloom. Also, aphids become more of a problem when roses are parched, so it's important to water regularly without letting the soil become soggy. Pots and planters should have drainage holes at the bottom to allow excess water to run off; the container can stand on a saucer or a plate if the floor damages easily. If you prefer to use containers without drainage holes to avoid soiling the floor, place a 5 cm to 10 cm (2' to 4') layer of Leca clay pebbles at the bottom of the pot or planter; that way the water can pool at the bottom of the pot without damaging the roses as much. Outside containers that are not protected by a roof overhang must

Potted roses and miniature roses are excellent container summer plants, here with spurge 'Diamond Frost'.

A 'Dronning Margrete' rose as foundation rose with Swan River daisies around its base. At the front is the 'Aloha' rose planted in the flowerbed.

Soil shrinks with watering, and must be topped up as needed.

have drainage holes; if not, the container will fill up with water during heavy rains, and the plant roots will suffocate.

Roses need a lot of water, and during the blazing days of summer you may want to give them extra to drink. When it rains, however, you'll need to empty out the water that collects in the saucer so the rose doesn't become waterlogged. A rose that droops—even if the soil is only moist—is a rose that has received too much water. You can save it by leaning the container to drain out the excess water, but it won't be easy. Another option is to remove the plant from the waterlogged container and settle it into another pot, but it will still take a while to recover.

Several years in container

Roses that aren't hardy can be grown as container plants and be saved from year to year. This is common practice in the north of Sweden where the selection of hardy roses is limited. Container roses are more often afflicted by fungal disease than other roses however, so mixing an organic treatment like Swedish Bio-Balans (or similar) in with the container's soil is recommended. Many professional rose breeders do this to safeguard their flowers.

Use the best soil that you can find to fill your containers. The soil has to be stable; using discounted outlet soil is not advisable. You can buy special soil for roses, or custom soil for potted plants. The soil is not allowed to settle too far down or dry out to the point where it pulls away from the side of the pot. You can mix your purchased bagged soil with a third or a fourth of garden soil, if the ground soil is in good shape. Composted soil is a good choice for the rose container, as it gives plants a boost and keeps them healthy. Even a container rose's bud union (see p. 15) has to be planted 5 cm to 10 cm (2" to 4") below the surface of the soil.

Violets and roses do not make a harmonious combination in a flowerbed; they're challenging to care for and they don't bloom at the same time. With container plantings, however, feel free to mix it up. Here, roses are paired with violet-blue, small-flowering pansies that bloom over a long stretch of time, and honey-scented sweet alyssum.

Protect container roses by burying them in the ground, pot and all. Cover them with porous soil, fall leaves, and twigs to keep the leaves in place.

Tree rose with companion plant moneywort.

Overwintering container roses

The most difficult aspect of growing roses in containers is overwintering them. Even if the roses are hardy they'll freeze more quickly when planted in containers because their roots are sensitive to cold, and in winter the air gets colder than the ground. Roses should not be kept too warm or too cold; a few degrees above or below freezing works best. They can cope at a few degrees below freezing, but not too many degrees and not for too long. The temperature should be kept as steady as possible, or else the plants might be fooled into starting growing too early, after which they'll freeze in the next cold snap. An unheated garage, a glassed-in balcony or deck with a temp-regulating frost sensor, or better yet, a root cellar, are all good places to set a container rose in winter.

Container roses can stay outside in winter if they're adequately protected. They can be set close together in a corner next to a warm wall. First, protect the roots, as they are the least hardy part of the plant. You can dig a hole and set the entire pot in the ground, and cover the hole with leaves. If you don't want to bury the pot, remove it and set in only the root ball. Another way to protect the rose is to cover the pot with straw

or other insulating material (which must be kept dry).
Place the pot in a box to keep the insulation in place. The
container should stand under a roof overhang to keep the
insulation material dry, because if it becomes wet it will
freeze solid to ice. If the container can't be kept under the
roof, choose insulation material that is impermeable; that
is, it lets water slide off and away from the container, such
as plywood sheeting, a plastic tray or bag, fir branches or
the like. Keep in mind that you should not wrap the whole
plant in plastic, as air needs to circulate around it. The
soil must be moist when the container is put away—not
dry, but also not wet. If you can, check on the plant in late
winter and early spring; do not let the soil dry out.

Potted Tree Roses (Standards)

Tree roses (rose standards) make highly suitable container
plants, as they're more delicate than common roses.
Even if the rose at the top of the trunk is a hardy one, like
'The Fairy', it's still more delicate when grown as a tree.
In winter, rose trees need to be covered or placed in a
protected spot, preferably both. Containers are convenient
here, as they can be moved to an unheated garage or other
protected area when the cold arrives. Wrap a few layers of
burlap around the foliage crown at the top of the trunk;
the spot where trunk and the canes meet is especially
sensitive. If you don't want the pot to show during the
summer, dig it down into the flowerbed, and then dig it up
again in the fall.

You can find some potted flowering roses on the
market that have been grown farther south. Typically
these are varieties that are not very hardy where we live,
but they can still be very striking as container plants. They
flower flamboyantly during the summer and fall, but have
trouble surviving the winter. If the name on the label is
unknown and the text is in German, Italian, or French,
chances are the rose is less hardy.

*Tree roses can be used as summer flowers in containers. These
can be varieties of bedding roses sold as standards, or complete
unknowns. If the names of the roses are unfamiliar, you can
assume that they are not hardy. Here are three roses braided
together to form a trunk with a multicolored crown. In the
foreground is a dahlia in bud and several kinds of grandiflora
petunias.*

Some garden centers specialize in roses and keep a large assortment of them in stock.

ROSES IN GARDEN CENTERS AND IN CULTIVATION

Many people think of roses as fussy and demanding plants; consequently the sales of roses, as well as interest in the plant itself, have diminished. This is unwarranted, however, since the bloom of modern roses is both long lasting and prolific, granting it a well-deserved spot in the garden. They're neither difficult to care for nor challenging if they're planted correctly, but it can be difficult to find the right rose.

Rose breeding has produced many fine and enchanting specimens. There are a few garden centers in Sweden that specialize in roses, but none make available all the interesting and suitable varieties that thrive specifically in Sweden. You can special order those specific roses at garden centers (who in turn order them directly from the grower) to be delivered in early spring or fall. You can also shop for roses online. Bare-root roses (see p. 138) ship easily, and are not harmed by spending a few days in transit with the postal service. If you're looking for a specific rose to buy, you'll need to start looking early, because rose plants take a long time to get ready for sale; if you're unlucky in your timing, you may have to wait a whole year before the next batch is ready. As with almost anything, you also have to take into consideration the laws of supply and demand; new varieties are trickier to find and can therefore be expensive. Bare root roses, on the other hand, can be ordered in the fall just after the harvest, when there's a wide selection to choose from. Many don't dare to plant roses in the fall, thinking they might freeze over the winter. The opposite holds true, however, since roses planted in the fall often survive the winter better than those already in the ground. When a rose is planted, it's set deeply in the ground and is fully covered up. An older rose may not have the same amount of protection, since soil has a tendency to settle and sink over time; it may look as though the rose is creeping up and out of the soil, its root becoming more visible and exposed as years pass. In order to protect the roses, you have to take care to add more soil around them each year (see more about 'Rose care,' p. 15.)

Quality

Roses that are grown and bundled together to be sold in supermarkets are often older specimens. They're less expensive to buy because they no longer command a license fee, and they're produced in developing countries where the cost of labor is low. If you prefer newer or more exotic varieties of top-notch quality, you'll have to shop for your flowers at a garden center or a nursery. You do get what you pay for, so there are rarely any bargains to be found. A good plant should have at least three sturdy canes, each growing in a different direction. The canes will be more or less thick, depending on the type of rose. If the roots are free of soil, they should show a lot of fine light threads, not just one or two coarse sticks.

Bare-root or potted plants

Roses can be sold as bare-root plants, or as grown in containers, or somewhere in the middle—potted up. Bare-root is the most affordable option; the rose is dug up from the soil while dormant, and is kept cool and damp to prevent the roots from drying out. Roses that are not sold in the fall are kept in special cold storage, and are sold the following spring. A garden center or nursery specializing in roses can sell bare-root roses that they keep in a cooler, which prevents the roses from starting to grow; they remain viable and can be sold in April and May. Once the rose is removed from cold storage, however, it needs to be planted with as little delay as possible.

Garden centers and nurseries use different methods to preserve the health of the rose; some pack the rose roots in bags of peat moss to prevent them from drying out, and also apply wax to the roses' canes to keep them moist.

Roses that are stored in bags are easy to handle; they can be laid flat in boxes and sent out without a problem as long as they're kept cool. When the rose—its roots packed in a plastic bag—arrives at the point of sale, it needs to be sold as quickly as possible. If the rose is left in a warm environment for a week or two, it will start greening up even if it's not planted; that's not good for the plant, and the salesperson should strike it off the inventory. Occasionally, roses are sold with budding leaves; with a bit of luck the rose might still make it, but it's not a plant I would recommend buying.

Due to the issue of premature budding described above, roses are now commonly packed and shipped in pots filled with peat moss instead of in plastic bags. The roses are then potted up in soil at the retail outlet, and can remain in those pots until they're sold. They're watered if they start

Roses are usually sold potted up—there's a difference between roses grown in containers and roses that have been potted up. Here are container-grown tree roses (rose standards) 'Leonardo da Vinci'. The layer of coconut fibers keeps the soil damp and controls weeds.

Roses vary widely in color, depending on influences such as weather and where they're grown. They're much easier to appreciate when you see them up close in real life. There are several lovely rosarium displays and rose gardens to visit in Sweden.

to grow, but they usually sell before they've had a chance to take root and start budding.

Flowering container plants

Roses grown in containers are not the same as roses potted up for sale. Container grown roses are planted in large pots filled with good soil, and are then left to grow and develop. They're planted early in spring and are delivered to retail outlets once they've taken root and begin to turn green. There's great demand for flowering, container-grown roses during the summer, but they can be quite pricey because green plants take up a lot of space in transport. Be that as it may, if you want to be absolutely certain to get a rose in your choice of color, container grown roses are the way to go. Sadly, options are very limited. If there's high demand for one type of rose, it will be removed—often in the fall— and be sold as a bare-root rose soon after it's been dug up, and before it's had a chance to be potted.

Affordable or pricey

Compare the price of roses that are for sale. Roses should be planted in deep pots preferably, so the bud union (where it's grafted) is down in the soil. The bigger the pot, the deeper the soil, and the more expensive the rose will be. There'll be an appreciable gap in price between a rose in a 2 liter (2 quart) pot and a rose in a 5 liter (5 quart) pot.

Big roses that have grown in containers for several years—climbing roses, for instance—can often reach more than 1 m (3.25') in height, and have an immediate visual impact. They can't compare to a bare-root rose wrapped in a plastic bag, even if they happen to be the same type of rose. A rose that has been grown in a container can look a bit mangy at the store; the soil gets dry and warm quickly in small pots, so the rose dries out and pests and diseases have an easier time gaining a foothold—see 'Container roses,' p. 128. Once planted in a flowerbed or a large planter, however, the rose will perk up and look healthy again.

Tree roses (standards)

Tree roses, or standards as they're also called, are laborious to grow and awkward to move, but they are oh-so-beautiful. When buying one, make sure that the trunk is sturdy; the stronger the trunk the more stable the tree. Even when robust, however, the tree will need a stake for support along the trunk up into the crown. The height of the tree can vary, but one guiding principle is that the shorter the trunk, the less expensive the tree will be. There's a huge difference between a 40 cm to 60 cm (1.30' to 2') tree and one that is 1 m (3.25'). They make completely different impressions.

If you'd like a tree rose that can overwinter successfully, you'll have to buy a good-quality standard with a stable trunk. The tree's flowers also need to be hardy in the zone it's being planted in. Roses that are sold as tree roses are identical to roses for the flowerbed. If their variety is unknown, be wary of them and assume that they may not be a hardy specimen. They can, however, be used for summer blooms.

Where to buy roses

I recommend that you buy roses from your local garden center or nursery, as the employees will be familiar with all the quirks of the local environment and climate. Not all garden centers show the same interest in roses, however, so search the Internet or look up Svenska Rosensällskapet (The Swedish Rose Society) to find a good nursery in your area. Plantskolan Cedergrens (Cedergren's Nursery), in Råå, Helsingborg, Sweden, has sold roses by mail order for many years by now; their selection is excellent and they're thoroughly knowledgeable about roses. They also sell many varieties of clematis, for those who'd like to create companion plantings for their roses to prolong the flowering season.

Flora Linnea is a newer shop that is connected to the Fredriksdal Rosarium, a rose garden in Helsingborg, Sweden. They carry a large selection of both old and modern rose varieties. Many other garden centers and nurseries in Sweden sell a wide stock of roses, places like Åsby in Hallsberg, Bürgers in Köping, and Rydlinge in Skellefteå, to name just a few. So you don't have to throw in the towel simply because you can't find your preferred roses locally. The roses are available, but you may have to find a vendor who will accept special orders.

Buying roses from abroad, and dealing with name confusion

When reading about roses in foreign and/or translated books and catalogues, or visiting garden centers abroad, you'll get the impression that there are a lot of new roses out there. Of course, there are many German, English, and French varieties that are not for sale in Sweden, but not all of them. Many roses take on new identities in different countries and that creates a certain amount of confusion, but it's worth the effort to look up the correct name and classification of interesting varieties that you'd like to try. Information is available on the Internet, or in the Combined Rose List, which is also accessible online. It can be highly frustrating to haul an unusual and beautifully striped 'Christopher Columbus' all the way home from vacation, only to discover that Swedish garden centers have had this plant in stock since 2002, but it is sold under its real name 'Candy Cover'.

When reading catalogues and books about roses, do take all claims of hardiness with a grain of salt. The authors aren't misleading you intentionally, but they cannot be familiar with the vagaries of everyone's particular climate zones. A few well-known and highly respected authors believe that 'New Dawn' (Sweden Zone 5), 'Alchemyst' (Sweden Zone 3) and 'Händel' (Sweden Zone 2) are all vigorous growers and healthy climbers, and group them with climbers that can survive to -29°C (-20°F). This is irritating to someone from northern Sweden because it doesn't apply to those Swedish conditions at all. The same caution should be used when visiting rosariums in other countries—a rose isn't necessarily hardy because it survives cold winters in Germany. Flower sizes in foreign catalogues hardly ever match expectations either, so it's best to visit Swedish rose gardens to get an idea of what plants look like when growing in our climate.

A nicely packaged flowering rose from Holland. Its variety is unknown, so just assume it's not hardy in Sweden and use it as a summer flower.

Most of the roses sold in Sweden are grown in Fyn, outside Odense, in Denmark. The large field filled with rows upon rows of flowering roses is a striking sight. If a rose has ended up in the wrong place, it's immediately noticeable, since the smallest difference in shape and color stands out when so many of the same type are planted together.

BREEDING IN LARGE NUMBERS

At the French rose breeder Meilland, the process of hybridizing roses begins each year when 5,000 to 8,000 cultivars are crossbred through the hand pollination of 100,000 to 120,000 flowers. This produces a huge amount of rosehips. The seeds from the hips are then planted to grow approximately 250,000 young plants. These new plants are cultivated further, and go through an eight to ten-year long growth and selection process where each year more plants are rejected from the range. The final batch of plants is propagated through cuttings, and then test grown in fifteen different locations. In the end, approximately ten plants are picked as new roses to be introduced on the market. Each rose is protected by patent for twenty-five years. At present, Meilland owns 1,000 patents, i.e. 1,000 different kinds of roses that are available commercially; the company sells around twelve million rose plants a year

Rose gardens worth the trip

I'm sure you don't mind driving a few extra miles to check out a rose, especially if it's a special cultivar you've been yearning for. If you're happy with any red or yellow specimen, then you'll have it easy by simply picking out flowers among this book's many suggestions. If you have your mind set on a special flower, however, it'll be worth your while to see the rose in cultivation, in situ. There are many small rosariums—rose display gardens—and private gardens where you can take an up-close look at different varieties. Groupings of roses are helpfully tagged with nameplates in Swedish parks and castle gardens such as Skansen in Stockholm, the Norrvikens Gardens outside Båstad in Skåne (the southernmost province of Sweden), Bosjö Abbey (also in the south of Sweden), as well as at Himmelstalund School in Norrköping and Sofiero (once a Royal country mansion in Helsingborg).

Many garden centers and nurseries feature adjoining gardens for demonstrations and exhibits, perhaps in collaboration with a local gardening society. Ask around to discover the hidden gems that may be found in the vicinity. Many garden societies, such as The Swedish Rose Society, as well as municipalities, organize garden visits and tours open to the public; look for further information on The Swedish Horticultural Society's homepage at www.tradgard.org, and at The Swedish Rose Society's website at www.svenskarosensallskapet.org. Old-fashioned rose blooms are at their most lavish in early July, so there are many showings. Modern roses bloom beautifully throughout July and August—often longer.

A grafted rose where the green canes are growing from the green 'eye', which is visible in the picture below. The brown segment is the root from which the rose is growing. At the time of planting, the point at which the green and brown parts meet—the bud union—should be placed between 5 cm to 10 cm (2" to 4") beneath the soil's surface. That way, true new shoots grow from the green canes instead of suckers from the brown stock root.

Grafted stock root where a true rose grows as a green shoot after the grafting. This shoot will later become a large rose.

The Garden Society of Gothenburg has an amazing rose collection, many of which are modern roses that bloom the entire summer. Fredriksdal Museum and Gardens in Helsingborg, in Skåne, boasts a rosarium full of old roses. They also keep some modern roses in a beautiful rose garden.

Jönköpings Rosarium is not as well known, but is still very good. It features mostly modern and climbing roses, which means that there are flowering roses even in the fall. The rosarium is located in Rosenlund next to interstate E4, near the Elmia Exhibition and Convention Center.

Wij Gardens in Ockelbo, in central Sweden (Sweden zone 5), has recently built a rosarium meant to showcase hardy roses. The bulk of their collection consists of old roses that only flower once. Sadly, a lot of the modern prolific bloomers are missing; it would have been interesting to see how their hardiness holds up.

Roses in cultivation

While species roses and garden roses are all kin, cultivated specimens are very much improved over species types. Roses have been cultivated for thousands of years, during which time the most beautiful flowers have been chosen and bred. Roses propagate by seed, and the progeny can vary significantly in appearance since not all the seeds from one rose hip will grow up to become identical plants. One single plant can look different, its traits having been selected and preserved already a thousand years ago. This was the beginning of rose breeding; over the last two hundred years, however, growers have gone about isolating desired characteristics in a more systematic way, which is why there are marked contrasts between roses today.

Roses are still bred the same way nature intends, but improvements to the end result are made far more methodically. Some types are crossed—hybridized—then the seeds are collected and sown. Aside from having seeds that yield natural variations, roses can also change genetically—produce mutations—due to natural causes. A cane with flowers of a different type or color can appear spontaneously. This new development is called a 'sport,' and many new varieties of roses materialize like this. When a new rose comes about in this way and is deemed suitable for further development, breeders use vegetative propagation—taking shoots or cuttings from the new rose to grow more of the same—since this is the only way to ensure a true, genetically identical copy.

Own-root or rootstock

Roses can be bred with cuttings, or grafting. If a cutting—a shoot from a cane—is taken and simply stuck in the ground, the plant that emerges will be true, grown from its own root. It might grow less vigorously than other roses; typically it'll develop more slowly and will be smaller in size. Due to this, roses in the industry are most often sold grafted onto another rose's root. The same goes for many ornamental bushes and fruit trees; they're not grown on their own roots.

Grafting

When roses are grafted, a small piece—a bud eye, also called a scion—is taken from a cane and inserted into another plant in order to use that plant's root. There are enormous advantages to using this technique,

An eye (scion) from the cultivar.

because even if the roses are of different types, they all grow at the same pace. Rootstock roses are grown from seed and are inexpensive to buy. Many more than are needed can be planted, and the excess discarded. Many more plants can be produced by using a rose for grafting than by only using it for cuttings. A cutting will need five to six 'eyes' whereas one eye is enough to produce a plant with grafting.

Grafting is a task often performed by horticulture specialists. From mid July to mid August, they make their way around Europe like a craftsman's guild and perform 'graftage.' If the grafting is done later or earlier in the season, it will be difficult for the graft to take, i.e. for the scion to attach itself to the stock root.

Many years

To breed roses, you first must have rose plants growing and available to use as rootstock, also called under-stock. Under-stock is typically a *Rosa canina* (dog rose) or a Japanese climbing rose, both of which propagate through seeds. The seeds are sown either in fall or spring in fields lined with shallow rows, and then covered with 1 cm to 2 cm (0.5" to 1") of sand.

In Year 1, once the seeds have germinated in spring, the plants are made to grow densely enough that they stretch upward in one long straight shoot. The plant is left to develop over the summer, and in the fall it's harvested and cleaned off, the root and shoot size trimmed off hard to develop a compact root system. The rootstock is then preserved in a cooler over winter, and then planted out as early as possible in the spring of Year 2. Many companies buy rootstock that's delivered in spring.

In the spring of Year 2, the rootstock is planted 15 cm to 20 cm (6" to 8") apart, and the soil is piled up around the upper section—the neck—of the root. In the summer, the top uppermost soil is removed and the neck is left bare over several weeks to encourage thicker bark formation before the grafting takes place.

The eye itself (the scion, the part that is to become the new plant) is taken from growing rose plants destined for retail outlets in the fall. The plants are cut while they're in the midst of their most beautiful bloom, and the pieces of cane are collected and used. (When the plants are in full flower it's easy to see if a different rose was mistakenly planted, or if an error was made while sorting, so that the unwanted plant can be easily removed.)

The eye is stripped so that some of the bark and underlying wood is attached. A very shallow T-cut is made in the neck of the rootstock and the scion is placed in the cut, wrapped securely with a rubber band or grafting tape to keep the scion in place. The plant is left in the field after the grafting to grow and develop further. In the fall of Year 2, soil is piled up around the plant to protect it over winter.

Once spring arrives in Year 3, the soil is removed again from around the base of the plant, and the canes are pruned off from the root. The cut is made above the upper edge of the T-cut, just above the fused eye. When the new shoot reaches 5 cm to 6 cm (2" to 2.5") it is topped; this is repeated once again before midsummer. The amount of topping is not the same for all types of roses; it all depends on how much they grow.

The plant is deadheaded once more in August, which helps to produce a sturdy, fully branched out plant. In the fall, it'll be time to harvest it once it begins to drop its leaves. The plant is dug up, its roots are trimmed and shortened, after which the bare-root plant is ready to be sold. Most of the plants are kept in a cooler, however, and are not sold until the following spring when demand is at its peak.

In the spring of Year 4, the roses are up for sale. Years ago it was common to sell them as bare-root plants, which meant they could only be planted in late fall after the harvest, or early in spring before shoots start appearing. Container-grown roses are planted in special, extra deep pots, in the spring of Year 4, and are then placed in growing beds. They're ready for sale when they have taken root in the pots and are starting to leaf out.

The soil is blown away to leave the root bare.

A cut is made in the root bark and the eye is placed below the bark.

The eye is in place.

The eye is wrapped with grafting tape, to keep it securely in place and to protect it from drying out.

Grafting is finished and the soil replaced.

A rootstock rose that has been allowed to grow; this type is used for some old-fashioned roses.

ROSE BREEDERS

There are many rose breeders in business today, but not as many as in the 19th century, when many non-professionals produced their own hybrid or two. Today's breeders are large companies that launch the majority of all new roses on the market, and keep their old ones going. They own the patent on the cultivar, and for each single plant that gets grafted the rose grower is required to pay a license fee to the owner company.

Breeders' aims have changed over time. Demand for color, shape, and size is swayed by fashion and fads, but roses don't change that quickly since it can take between fifteen and twenty years to produce a new variety. Today the goal is to produce roses with old-fashioned beauty that are healthier than their predecessors, with more abundant blooms and, most importantly, continuous flowering. There's also an eagerness to produce new, unconventional colors and combinations. The search for a blue rose is still on.

The future lies in producing carefree roses that are resistant to fungal diseases, hardy to withstand winter without protection, and well balanced and healthy enough to require very little pruning.

Own-root or rootstock

The root of the plant transfers some of its characteristics to the grafted rose. The dog rose (*Rosa canina*) root creates a hardy plant but a less prolific bloomer; it's used quite often as rootstock for old-fashioned roses. The Japanese climbing rose, *Rosa multiflora*, produces a more active bloomer and is the most commonly used rootstock in Sweden; it's seen in many gardens. If you let its suckers grow, they will often crowd out the grafted rose. A Japanese climber is recognizable by its beautifully glossy, bright green, yet quite small leaves, and its profusion of small white flowers the size of a buttercup. It has a climbing growth habit with long canes.

Be extra cautious when buying roses abroad, where another rootstock—*Rosa laxa*, which is less hardy—is often used. There are own-root roses for sale in Sweden and all over Europe, but more experience with them is still needed to assess their strength. You can take cuttings from them and grow your own plants, but don't count on their hardiness being reliable.

Not all roses destined for the marketplace are suitable to be grown on own root, but it may work in the home garden. If the rose is planted deep enough in the ground, the canes can root and produce their own-root plant. The shoots growing up around the plant are own-root and the same as the originating canes. Larger shrub roses and park roses produce their own roots, but even some bedding roses will do this. Roses from Poulsen will form own roots if they're planted deep in the soil, and eventually the rootstock will die off; what remains is the own-root rose.

It's important to add new soil every spring if you want your rose to produce own roots. The soil around the rose settles during the summer when its nutrients are being absorbed, so the root neck ends up exposed even if the root was planted deeply at the beginning.

Rose trees (standards)

Rose trees, also known as standards, are a special case; they're expensive to purchase and they're more challenging to cultivate. They consist of a rose plant affixed to the top of a tall trunk. As a rule, the root is one type of rose plant, the trunk is another, and the rose at the top yet another. In some rare instances the root and trunk are of the same stock.

The grafting is done the same way as on any other rose, except that the eye is inserted higher up towards the top of the trunk instead of at ground level. The trunk is quite weak and needs to be supported, and the support needs to extend all the way to the top of the tree.

A true own-root tree, i.e. the trunk and root are from the same plant, is unusual, but you can produce one at home. This tree rose calls for a strong growth habit and sturdy canes.

The point where crown and trunk joins is quite delicate, and should be covered up in winter. For that reason standards are less hardy than the same type of rose planted in the ground. In Denmark, growers use a trunk that is very hardy; in the Netherlands and England, however, other trunks are routinely used, which means that a plant's hardiness can vary according to the country of origin.

'Isabella Rosselini' is a new rose from the Danish rose breeder Poulsen. The same company bred 'Ingrid Bergman', a very popular bedding rose, which is now starting to show its age. This new rose is nearly identical to 'Ingrid Bergman', and is also an improvement on it. In ten to twenty years time, however, it will be time to look for a replacement for 'Isabella Rosselini', a replacement that does not exist yet.

Well-known rose breeders

European companies have launched most of the roses available for sale in Sweden; there are, however, a few American companies that have contributed to the selection. Below you'll find a list of some of the breeders of the most common roses in Sweden. The advantage of knowing the breeder's name is that they usually cultivate their own particular 'style'.

The three to four capital letters in the breeder name are the same first letters as in the plant's unique code name. If you know the code name then you'll know who bred the rose, so you'll be able to find out more information about it (the company usually posts information about their roses online). New roses are usually advertised in product groups or types of roses, but they are not true groups; they're more like collections. For example, the name English Roses or Castle Roses are trade names.

AUS is for the English Austin, which sets its sight on old-fashioned roses with fragrance and cupped flowers. Breeding started in the 1950s, and 'Constance Spry' was its first rose available commercially. Approximately four million Austin roses are sold each year.

BAI stands for the American Baily Nurseries, a plant nursery that has its own rose breeding operation. They're new to the rose breeding business, and focus their work on own-root roses with the concept of 'Easy Elegance Roses'. 'Mystic Fairy' and 'Golden Eye' are Bailey's own-root groundcovers that are beginning to sell in Sweden.

DEL is for the French company Delbard, which has very few roses that are hardy in Sweden. They launched the series called 'Rosiers des Peintres' (Painters' Roses) with, for example, 'Henri Matisse' and 'Camille Pissaro'. They are absolutely gorgeous but, sadly, not dependably hardy in our Swedish climate.

DIC is Dickson Roses from Northern Ireland, a 6th generation rose breeding family that have given us roses like 'Tequila Sunrise' and 'Elina'.

HAR means the English company Harkness, which started at the end of the 19th century. Their 'Amber Queen' and 'Alexander' are still popular.

KOR stands for the German firm Kordes, which offers quite hardy and healthy roses. Two well-known roses are 'Alchemyst' and

'Sommerwind'; a recent addition called Maxi is a collection of climbing roses. They also produce container roses.

MAC as for McCredy, which at first was Irish; they have now relocated to New Zealand. They have many fine specimens like 'Jan Spek', 'Matangi' and 'Penthouse', as well as bicolor roses. The company sells the right to name their products, so for a fee you can name a rose.

MEI stands for the French Meilland, a 6th generation family rose breeding firm that produced 'Peace'. They launch roses in different product groups, all very charming with fine fragrance. They also produce beautiful cutting roses for professional growers, as well as container roses.

NOA is German Noack, which looks to produce healthy roses. They have introduced an extremely fine rose series, 'Flower Carpet', which has met great success in the US.

POU stands for Danish Poulsen, which is known for healthy and hardy roses. 'Ingrid Bergman' and 'H.C. Anderson' are two of their flowers that are very well known.

TAN is German again, this time for Tantau in Uetersen, Germany. Among their many famous roses you'll find 'Super Star' (Tropicana) and 'Nostalgie'.

WEK is Weeks Roses in California and rose breeder Tom Carruth. We don't have any of his roses in Sweden, but in the US he is considered one of the best national rose breeders. They have produced several stripy roses.

Roses will flower up until the first snowfall; it's very beautiful, but not very smart from an overwintering perspective.

PROBLEM ROSES

Roses aren't as popular now as they were fifty years ago; many feel that they aren't hardy anymore and that their quality has declined. This may be correct in some cases, but if roses tend to catch diseases or freeze more frequently nowadays, it may have more to do with climate change than with the quality of the plants. Location, soil, and care are all factors in how well roses cope with colder weather. Some roses are more demanding, some are less so, and they all react differently to fungal diseases. Pick the right rose, however, and you'll steer clear of a lot of trouble.

We have four seasons, and in the cold of winter roses are not meant to grow; in order to survive that time of year they need to go dormant. In the fall, the plant reacts to the gradual cooling in temperature by thickening its cells' walls, a process called 'hardening off.' The canes stop growing, the leaves drop, and the ends of the canes close up and become tough. The amount of water in the plant decreases substantially; if there's too much water in the cane the cold will freeze and destroy it. The rose stays dormant until spring.

Hardy or not

Many plants that are hardy in Sweden—birches, for instance—grow according to the length of the day, that is, they prepare for dormancy when days begin to shorten. In the spring they don't respond to warmth, even when the temperature is well above freezing. They are not ready to awaken because the days are still too short.

Roses, by contrast, are more influenced by temperature. If the fall is drawn out and warm they'll continue to flower into November and even December. While it's great to be able to enjoy their beauty a little longer, the downside is that the roses become more susceptible to freezing. Non-remontant roses that flower only once don't suffer too much harm, as they start to slacken off soon after their blooming period is over. Continuously flowering roses don't have this tapering-off period, however; they just keeping blooming, and absorbing water and nutrients for their flowers, until it gets cold. When the weather turns, the canes are still full,

If the rose is set in too shallow, the green canes will freeze down to the ground and there will be no more own-root rose to send up new shoots; the shoots will instead be suckers from the rootstock. This picture shows the red bedding rose 'Allotria' in the company of its root (or stockroot, as it's appropriately called), which is the Japanese climbing rose Rosa multiflora. Here they're in luck because part of the grafted rose is still there, but eventually the Japanese climber will take over and be the only one left.

juicy, and green with buds at the end; they're not in the least prepared to go dormant, so they do get injured when it starts to freeze at night.

Once they've stopped flowering and have entered dormancy, they tend to overreact on an unexpected warm day; they believe spring has sprung so the sap in the plants start running and their buds swell. When the cold inevitably returns, the roses freeze again and are further damaged. A cycle of warm days and cold nights can take place several times in spring, during which time roses can take a real beating if they're not protected.

If you're in luck, only the leaves and buds freeze, but if you're not, the canes may freeze all the way to the ground. If the rose isn't own-root, the big risk is that only shoots from the rootstock will grow in spring. It's quite common that rootstock shoot—suckers—take over because the grafted rose died from the cold, especially with climbing roses.

Non-remontants (non-repeater) roses

Roses that bloom once or twice are usually hardier than their continuously flowering counterparts. A rose that stops blooming in July is better equipped to handle winter than a rose that continues to flower through the whole summer. Non-remontant roses, also called non-repeaters, are therefore the hardiest roses and the best suited to colder climates.

Alas, if it were only that simple. As it is, not all non-remontants are hardy; it depends also on how they bloom. Some roses flower on last year's growth, like early flowering shrub roses and many of the climbers—'Flammentanz', for instance. The problem here is that the canes can freeze in the winter and then produce no flowers at all. Granted, the canes are rather frost hardy and seldom freeze, but that depends on the type of rose, too.

Roses that flower on new growth that emerges within the year will bloom later in the summer. Their advantage is that flowering shoots growing out new each year can't be damaged by the cold, so they're often considered hardy. Their main drawback, however, is that they may get a late start and bloom late in the season. Some roses bloom on both the past year's as well as the current year's growth, making it difficult to judge their hardiness.

Good soil is key

While hardiness is somewhat contingent upon what type of rose you're dealing with, it depends much more on where the rose is planted and what kind of soil it's planted in. The rose will freeze far more easily in a heavy, damp clay soil where the ground frost enters deeply, than in a sandy soil where water drains away. Roses need lots of water and nutrients, but they can't live in wet soil. Occasionally it is postulated that roses do well in clay soil, but that's only part of the story. Clay soil is good only if it's easily crumbled and dug so the water can drain through it. You'll recognize clay soil if you can form patties with it by rolling it between the palms of your hands; a heavy clay soil can form very thin ropy sausages. When planting in clay soil, you'll have to dig extra large planting holes and amend the soil by mixing in an equal amount of compost to make it more friable.

Roses fare better in sandy soil, but water drains away too quickly for it to provide adequate moisture for optimum growth in summer, so you'll need to water the flowers several times a week. Sandy soil needs to be mixed with equal amounts of compost, cow manure or commercial soil to become moister and more nutrient rich.

Yet, no matter how hardy they are, all roses will die in waterlogged soil. Perform a test by digging a planting hole and filling it with water. The water should drain within a few hours. If the water is still there after 24 hours with no precipitation, however, you'll need to drain the hole and amend the soil properly before it can be used for any kind of cultivation.

Mild winters

When winter weather vacillates between warm and cold and there's no protective snow cover, roses tend to freeze. The trouble lies in the abrupt change in temperature; the canes thaw and start sprouting, then the cold returns and the roses freeze. This is why it's good to pile soil up around the rose plants and cover the canes of climbing roses. In areas where there's plenty of snow, place fir branches on the plant and let the blanket of snow provide the remaining coverage. In milder climates, pile soil around the plants and cover them with twigs, branches, leaves, or other dry materials.

Sick roses

Many gardeners consider roses to be nothing but trouble as far as disease is concerned. If you pick the right roses and look after them properly, however, you can avoid a lot of heartache. Any plant—not only roses—will be far more resistant to disease if it feels good where it grows. Roses don't become hardier when deprived of water and nourishment; quite the contrary. If they're to do well, then they need plenty of water and nutrients throughout the summer. A rose that is planted in the wrong soil or in an unsuitable location, or that isn't receiving the water and

Bedding roses need to be pruned each spring, and soil has to be piled up around them each fall. In this picture the root has emerged aboveground. Consequently, the grafted rose will easily freeze and leave the rootstock free to send up suckers.

nutrients it needs, is a rose that's not going to feel well. It will freeze or fall prey to disease, or both, no matter what type of rose it is. Most of the damage done to roses is by fungal diseases and garden pests, but they can be fought in several ways. Sadly, there are no miracle cures or shortcuts to be found in these pages; it mostly boils down to types of roses and proper care.

All roses are vulnerable to pest attacks

Even the hardiest roses can be attacked or become infested, since they're all vulnerable to pests. It has very little to do with what type of rose it is; the culprit is often its location, the weather and wind, and general care. An exception can be made for pollen beetles, which prefer light yellow, yellow, and light pink roses. Yellow is their preferred color and they typically visit the colza fields, but some years see too many of them and they end up in the garden flowers instead. The severity of the attacks can vary from year to year, but there's really no way to avoid them.

Flying pests

Aphids are very common pests. They sit in large clusters on the buds, as well as on the upper and undersides of tender leaves. Start by crushing the insects with your fingers, and then spray them off the plants with water. When most of them have been removed by hand, you can spray the plant

It's important to choose healthy roses. Newer varieties are typically more resistant to fungal diseases like powdery mildew than older ones.

with an organic, non-toxic insect treatment once a week for at least three consecutive weeks. The aphids give birth to live young, but they also reproduce by eggs that hatch. You can't get rid of them entirely, as they are all around us, and they also provide food for small birds. Their numbers can be controlled, but with aphids you just have to accept that there always will be a few of them around.

Aphids impede the rose's growth, causing the leaves and flowers to become deformed when they suck the sap from them. Aphids also excrete honeydew, a sweet, sticky secretion, onto the rose leaves; fungal spores grow into this secretion. They look like black mold and deplete the plant's energy to grow and flower.

Whiteflies are a form of lice; they're white and quick, and show up on leaves very clearly. They're fought in the same way you'd deal with aphids, but since they move swiftly it's difficult to home in on and spray-treat them.

Thrips pierce roses and leave tiny pinpricks behind. Flowers can become riddled with pinpricks, and with sustained attacks the leaves can be more or less destroyed. As a result, the rose grows badly and produces fewer flowers. Thrips are difficult to ward off since they're also very quick, which makes it challenging to hit them with a treatment spray. They're an especially common problem for roses that are grow in a protected spot—against a sunny house wall, for example.

Larvae

Aside from aphids, thrips and whiteflies—all flying insects that wreak havoc on rose plants—there are other harmful insects to watch out for. First there are larvae from the flying insects, which can be very tricky to get rid of. Larvae stay well protected by rolling themselves inside leaves or by sitting on the canes, so the most effective way to treat this infestation is by hand. Pick or cut off any rolled up, damaged leaves and eaten buds. There are several other insects that inflict similar kinds of damage; they're described in the text below. It isn't really necessary to remember which insect caused the damage, however, as the treatment method is the same, i.e. remove the leaf or shoot that looks damaged or strange.

Rose leafhoppers manifest themselves as larvae, eggs, and full-grown adult insects. Affected leaves are dotted with many small, yellowish white spots; the leaves eventually dry up and fall off the plant. The eggs are laid under the bark on young canes in the fall. In the spring the larvae sit on the underside of the leaves and feast on them. A rose leafhopper infestation is treated by cutting off the affected canes. You can also use insect spray or pyrethrum on the visible larvae.

Tortix, or leafroller moths, are really several kinds of butterflies whose larvae rip and eat the rolled up rose leaves from within. It's difficult to get to the larvae; nevertheless, as soon as you spy any rolled-up leaves, pick them off the plant and crush them.

Shootborer sawflies make young shoots wither suddenly. The shoot bends down to make a U shape, and wastes away. The larvae are inside the shoot, so it must be cut off to remove the pests. If not, the larvae will overwinter in the soil and begin their damage anew in the spring.

Leafrolling sawflies make the edges of the rose leaves roll in length-wise; the damage is easy to spot. Remove all affected leaves and crush the eggs sitting along the leaves' edges. Not all rolled up leaves contain eggs, but remove them all anyway to be on the safe side. The eggs hatch later to produce larvae that are about 1 cm (½") long, thin and white, and that live inside the rolled-up edge of the leaf.

Roseslug sawflies are larvae that eat the surface of the leaf. They often sit on the plant's lower leaves, while other insects are usually found on the tops of shoots. The affected leaves roll up, dry up, and fall to the ground. The larvae overwinter in the ground below the plant, and resume their attack the following year. The larvae are just over 1 cm (½") long and translucent. Crush them or spray them with a treatment.

Banded rose sawflies also produce larvae that eat the top area of the leaf. The larvae can be easily seen, but they don't inflict too much damage. They're about 1 cm (½") long or more, green with small, reddish brown heads, and they roll themselves up when disturbed. They're ugly and a nuisance, but are not especially dangerous to the plant.

Bedeguar gall wasp is a mouthful of a name for an insect that many of us have seen and wondered about. It's what's responsible for the moss-like, odd growths we notice on some leaves, flowers, and buds; they're quite commonly seen on wild species roses. The wasps cause no great harm to the rose, but do cut off the growth when it starts to turn brown.

Rose leafhopper is like an aphid, an indiscriminate eater when it comes to roses. Good care like regular pruning, and possibly a treatment with an organic horticultural insect spray, is the way to thwart this insect.

The tortix or leafroller moth is dealt with by hand. As soon as you see the rolled up, folded leaves where the larvae live, pick them off and crush them.

Aphids are the bane of roses. Water the plants regularly to prevent them from drying out, and blast the aphids with water as soon as they appear. Use full water pressure, and treat them repeatedly with a horticultural spray if necessary. It's also very easy to pick the lice off the plants with your fingers and crush them.

Large animals

Deer can be a nuisance. They love tender juicy shoots, and rosebuds are a particular delicacy. They will eat the rosebuds, even if there's other food available, simply because they find buds to be so tasty. Deer need to be frightened off, primarily with blood meal and, in Sweden, with a product called 'Mota Vilt' (an equivalent to the US's 'Repels-All') which contains citrus oils and other plant extracts; the same product also wards off rabbits and other game. Voles and moles are trickier; you can get special mole repellents that emit high-pitched sounds and vibrations that are inaudible to everyone but those animals. They can be wired up or be battery-powered. Either way, they work quite well.

Insecticides

Insects are treated first with insecticides that work on contact. Contact in this context means that it needs to hit the insect in order to be effective. Earlier, it was common to use systemic, all-in-one insecticides that infused the entire plant; the insect only had to taste a leaf to be put out of action. Pyrethrum is an organic, systemic product that can be used on roses, but as far as rose treatments go, insecticide is recommended first and foremost.

There are many plant treatments on the market. Some contain mineral oil, soft carbolic soap, or soap that's effective on both fungal disease and aphids. All spray products have to hit the insects in order to work, so be sure to cover the plant's buds, tops and undersides of leaves. Repeat this application about once a week. However, before applying any treatment, try washing off as many insects as possible with a high-pressure spray of lukewarm water first. Once the plant's foliage has dried, apply treatment to the plant.

Remember that plant treatments and chemical insecticides will affect all insects, whatever their size, so never spray bees, butterflies or other useful insects and pollinators. Also, never spray your plants in full sunshine, as the leaves will end up scorching. Chemical treatments are applied the same way as natural organic plant treatments.

Be proactive to prevent diseases

The biggest headache in growing roses is dealing with fungal diseases such as black spot, powdery mildew, and rose rust. How sick the plants become depends on their care, and on current weather conditions, but mostly on what type of rose you're dealing with. Black spot, powdery mildew, and rose rust can be prevented if you're proactive in caring for them. If you know that the plants typically get spotty leaves, spray them with treatment before the spots have the opportunity to reappear. If the plant still gets sick, pick off the leaves by hand, clean the area, and then spray it with an appropriate treatment (there are chemical treatments available, but I don't recommend using them). What roses are hardest hit by diseases depends on what country they grow in. It's a fool's errand to grow the climbing rose 'New Dawn' in certain areas of Skåne, in the south of Sweden, because it will develop powdery mildew as early as June. In central Sweden and farther north, however, that same rose is superbly hale and hearty. To maximize your success in growing healthy roses, ask people at the local plant nursery about their experience with different varieties of roses.

One way to keep roses in good condition is to prunc thcm hard. If most of the cane is removed there will be less room for diseases and insects to overwinter in. That's why climbing roses often run in to deep trouble: their long canes remain untouched from year to year. Their close-knit canes make sheltered nooks and crannies in walls and trellises for damaging insects to overwinter in.

Very full buds can rot if it's rainy and damp. Cut those buds off if they turn brown; they'll never recover. Water the roses with a drip hose, instead of a sprinkler hose or a showerhead, to avoid soaking the buds and flowers. It'll be easier on you, it's better for the flowers, and it uses up less water as well.

Weather and fungal disease

Fungal diseases don't affect all roses equally hard. The specimens suggested in this book are relatively new and still pretty resistant to diseases. By the same token, they're also so new that it's not easy to foresee their long-term health. Color can influence sensitivity. For example, apricot/orange roses can be more susceptible to disease than the light pink ones; frail pale blue types are also more easily infected.

The weather plays a part, too, in how likely roses are liable to catch a disease. A wet, rainy and cold summer will bring on more black spot, while a warm and dry summer will abet more powdery mildew. Fungal spores freeze in cold winters, which is why roses seem more immune to problems further up north.

Weather contributes more problems than fungal disease. Very full roses might have difficulty opening up completely when it's rainy, even when there is a drought, in which case the buds just rot or dry up. If it's excessively rainy some roses turn ugly from grey mold; by trimming off the withered flowers you can decrease the risk of spreading the mold to the rest of the blooms.

A rose that is healthy is more disease resistant. Poor levels of nutrients and water, inadequate soil, waterlogged sites, a cold climate, too much shade and rain, all increase the risk of roses developing a problem. Those that flower continuously through the summer need more water and nutrients than a rose that flowers only once. If they're not fed and irrigated properly, chances are they'll be less healthy and catch something; it follows that old-fashioned, non-repeating roses are healthier than bedding roses because they don't need as many nutrients or as much irrigation. Roses that have glossy dark leaves are usually more disease resistant than the type with soft grey/green leaves.

When it's time to switch roses

When foliage is infected by fungal disease it's no longer of any use. It can't provide the plant with nutrients and water so the plant becomes weak; even if it's still blooming, the flowers won't be all that attractive. Many times a diseased rose is saved because it still produces flowers, but it seldom improves. It might be possible to stop the fungus from causing more damage, but you cannot press the rewind button on what has already happened to the rose. It's better to remove the sick rose and plant a new, different variety.

Rose breeders produce hardy roses with good fungal disease resistance, but nature keeps fighting us. When a rose loses its resistance to disease or pests, its protective barrier is broken and so it easily becomes infected. This is the time to replace a problem rose with a new type, and keep the fight going year after year. The red bedding rose 'Nina Weibull' was very good when it was first introduced; roses that followed were 'Montana', and 'Pussta'. Today, 'H.C. Andersen' or 'Kensington' are recommended instead. The assortment of roses is usually quite good at garden centers, while big box stores sell mostly older bedding roses.

Fungal diseases

Black spot will take down almost any rose; a more pertinent question is how early in the season it'll happen. Leaves develop small black spots that grow progressively larger, after which the leaf turns yellow and drops off. If

this happens in the fall, things are progressing naturally for that time of year and all is well. It's not normal, however, for a rose to become sick as early as June or July. Black spot can be treated with organic plant treatments, a thorough cleanup around and on the plant, and pruning.

Powdery mildew is common in the south of Sweden—it's been on the increase since the climate has become milder. The fungus looks like a white coating on the foliage, which rolls up as it becomes infected. You can remove powdery mildew from the plant by cutting off everything that's been in contact with the fungus, and burning it, or throw it in the garbage. Using an organic plant treatment spray can lessen the infestations too.

Rose rust is a real challenge to deal with. It shows up as large orange spots on both the upper and underside of leaves. If the rose is not rare or isn't a plant that holds sentimental value, remove it and throw it in the thrash. Rose rust is common in the south of Sweden and has also increased in frequency due to milder winters. There's no effective treatment for rose rust other than removing all the infected leaves.

Black spot can be prevented through regular irrigation and fertilizing, because ailing plants tend to get sick more easily.

Disease resistant roses are the best defense against powdery mildew, black spot, and rose rust. Some years, however, the weather's influence is strong enough to have a detrimental effect on all types of roses, not just all of one particular species. If a rose becomes infected repeatedly, just remove it.

There are chemicals available to treat roses, but I don't recommended using them if you want your garden to be a haven for everybody. Instead, console yourself with the thought that birds enjoy eating aphids. Many flying insects deposit eggs that eventually become larvae that inflict damage on roses. However, some of them are truly beautiful, and many of them end up being a tasty treat for other, larger garden critters.

Organic treatments

You can turn to more eco-friendly treatments to combat fungal diseases, which means that you use nature's own methods to deter attacks and infestations. In Sweden, a product called BioBalans, (Bio-Cure-F is a similar product found in the US) is mixed into the soil around the rose plant each year; it contains four strains of Trichoderma fungus, as well as poultry manure, which lessen fungal disease attacks and encourage the roses to grow better. BioBalans is used in several rosariums in Sweden with great success. The Garden Society in Gothenburg, Sweden, grows its roses totally organically, i.e. without any chemicals; they mix BioBalans into the surface of the soil around the rose plant three times over the growing season. While on a visit to the Garden you can find out how the different roses

resist infection from fungus diseases. Even if outcomes vary due to the weather from year to year, all plants begin growing under the same conditions, which makes them easy to track and compare. Trichoderma fungus exists naturally in composted soil (just not in the same quantity as in BioBalans), which is why it's an excellent idea to use compost to amend your garden bed soil.

The struggle against damaging insects and animals is taken on quite swiftly by nature itself. Ladybugs and other insects are beneficial to the garden, so lure them to the roses by using companion plantings with your roses that the insects are attracted to. Lavender, hyssop, wood sage, and thyme are some favorite plants, but many other herbs are effective too. Avoid treatments and plant care products that kill beneficial insects at all costs.

Acknowledgments

A gardening book, especially one about roses, is nothing without its pictures. The photos herein were taken, for the most part, in private gardens throughout Sweden, as well as in a few rosariums. Some pictures even show allotments and home gardens that I noticed in passing, that I snapped without actually meeting their owners. So to all whom I didn't have the opportunity to meet personally and to express my gratitude, please accept my heartfelt thank you in this way.

Sincere kudos to all who create beautiful gardens that we all take delight in, whose invaluable contributions has made this volume a pictorial feast.

Much appreciation goes to my neighbors on the Swedish island of Hven, where the roses' luxuriance, health, and vigor inspire both awe and envy.

I'm indebted to Finn Eldh, a true enthusiast, for sharing from his extensive knowledge of all things clematis with me.

I'm ever grateful to Curt Rydlinge, Lena Truelsen, and other gardeners who so willingly shared their know-how on the cultivation of roses, especially in the northern part of Sweden.

Finally, sincere thanks to Grønløkke Plantskole, Peter Wallfält, Thomas Proll, and W. Kordes Söhne for availing themselves so generously to discuss and answer all my questions during the writing of this book.

Inger Palmstierna

Index of Roses

Plant Index

Index of Latin plant names